MW01093833

Monville

Forgotten Luminary of the French Enlightenment

Ronald W. Kenyon

CreateSpace
2013

The author has striven for accuracy and has endeavored to verify all factual information. All the opinions expressed herein are the author's, and he alone bears the responsibility for any errors in the text.

The illustrations in this book are reproductions of three engravings of the Désert de Retz after drawings by Constant Bourgeois (1767-1841), originally published in 1808 in *Le Nouveau Jardin Français* by Alexandre de Laborde.

Images courtesy of The Antiquarium, Houston, Texas.
Used with permission.

This book is available at quantity discounts for bulk purchase.
For information, please email the author at
rwkenyon@gmail.com.

Definitive edition

ISBN-13: 978-1481148290
ISBN-10: 148114829X

This book is dedicated to the memory of Jean-Louis Saury
July 21, 1933—October 15, 2012

Table of Contents

Preface

On December 21, 2007, it was with the utmost pleasure that I signed the deed transferring ownership of the Désert de Retz to the municipality of Chambourcy for the symbolic sum of one euro.

This was the end of the first act of a desperate combat I had maintained over several years to reopen the Anglo-Chinese garden created in the late eighteenth century by François Racine de Monville. This aristocrat, possessed of boundless curiosity, invested much of his fortune into this garden. He created from the ground up, on the edge of the Forêt de Marly, a place where nature was carefully arranged, and where rare trees and plants imported from all over the world scored counterpoint to pavilions and follies representing a number of civilizations in the history of humanity.

The visitor is invited to undertake an initiatory journey steeped in Masonic symbolism, a philosophical reflection on the universality of human thought and the desire for knowledge. Such a movement reached an apogee during the French Enlightenment. This secret place, far from the madding crowd, invites us to consider the impact of human activity on the environment through the inexorable flow of time.

The Broken Column is a clear reference to the Tower of Babel. The other buildings represent disparate cultures, all offspring of their common ancestor.

The originality of this work is that the author allows us to focus on François Racine de Monville, the man, recounting incidents in Monville's life that place him firmly in the midst of the social, political and cultural environment of the French Enlightenment.

It is my pleasure to invite the reader to visit Chambourcy to experience firsthand a marvelous and unforgettable voyage of the mind and the spirit—François Racine de Monville's legacy, the Désert de Retz.

> Dr. Pierre Morange
> Mayor of Chambourcy
> Deputy of Yvelines

Introduction

I discovered the Désert de Retz in 1973, while hiking in the Forêt de Marly[1] with a friend. Like many others—from Thomas Jefferson, Marie Antoinette and King Gustav III of Sweden in the 18th century to the novelist Colette, Jacqueline Kennedy Onassis, former President Jimmy Carter and the architect I. M. Pei in the 20th century—I was immediately enthralled by the garden. Subsequently, I conducted research in the Bibliothèque Nationale de France and in the collections of the Bibliothèque Municipale de Versailles to learn more about Monsieur de Monville and his "picturesque garden" in Chambourcy. In the following years I continued to visit the Désert de Retz, on occasion escorted by Jean-Marc Heftler-Louiche, then a co-owner of the property.

In 1996 I discovered the internet and immediately understood its potential: to make all human knowledge available to every person on the planet. I decided to create a website and asked myself if there was a subject about which I possessed enough knowledge to share with the rest of the world. The answer: Monsieur de Monville and his Désert de

---

[1] The Forêt de Marly is a 2,000-hectare (5,000-acre) forest estate in Yvelines, between Saint-Germain-en-Laye and Versailles about 15 km to the west of Paris. Historically, it was a royal hunting preserve.

Retz. The Racine de Monville Home Page[2] was born. The site receives an average of 10,000 page views per year from visitors in a hundred or more countries and has encouraged many people around the world to undertake the pilgrimage to Chambourcy to visit Monsieur de Monville's garden.

Over the years I have continued to augment and update the website on a regular basis. This book is an expansion of materials originally published on the website.

The primary purpose of this book is to make biographical information about Monsieur de Monville available to an English-speaking public. Diana Ketcham's excellent book, which attracted attention to the Désert de Retz, was published in 1997[3] and is now out of print.

Readers will notice an emphasis in the text on the Americans living in Paris at the end of the 18th century, many of whom might have known Monsieur de Monville or been his guests at his Paris townhouse or at the Désert de Retz. This trans-Atlantic focus is explained by the fact that Monville was one of many Frenchmen of his day who were supporters of American independence.

The French Enlightenment was a movement in the 18th century whose purpose was to reform society

---

[2] http://www.desertderetz.info

[3] Diana Ketcham visited the Désert de Retz again on June 26, 2009.

using reason, challenge ideas grounded in tradition and faith and advance knowledge through the scientific method.

From what we know of his accomplishments, Monville was a virtuoso musician on the harp and flute, a sportsman, an architect and an epicurean. As such, he was a quintessential representative of the French Enlightenment, a luminary among a constellation of luminaries. Unlike many of his contemporaries, however, he was largely forgotten until recently.

A partial explanation for Monsieur de Monville's fall into oblivion may be that no likenesses of him are known to exist. It is very easy to ignore someone whom you can't visualize. If, on the other hand, a portrait or a bust of Monville had survived, it would probably have been reproduced in the pages of French history books and on commemorative postage stamps.

I apologize for writing too much about Benjamin Franklin, who may not have met Monsieur de Monville. But Franklin's life in Paris was replete with anecdotes that will surely not fail to interest any student of the Franco-American relationship, and Franklin was as beloved and revered in France as he was in America: Monville displayed a terracotta medallion of Franklin in the Column House at the Désert de Retz.

I do not apologize, however, for devoting space to Émilie de Sainte-Amaranthe, acclaimed by many of her contemporaries as the most beautiful woman in France, whom Monville did know personally, and who perished on the guillotine at the age of nineteen, an innocent victim of the Reign of Terror.

Due to the paucity of documents relating to François Nicolas Racine de Monville and the lack of any of his personal papers or journals, I have taken the liberty of resorting to conjecture in numerous instances, basing my observations on circumstantial evidence. However, I have made scrupulous efforts to clearly differentiate between known facts and speculation, and have provided sources and references whenever possible. Because of the extensive nature of my research, I have also been able to correct some errors about Monsieur de Monville that have appeared elsewhere.

It is my conviction that much more remains to be discovered about François Racine de Monville and many of his secrets elucidated. To that end, I have written this biography, not only to inform and entertain, but to serve as a tool to facilitate the work of other researchers in the future.

Paris, October 2013

Acknowledgments

The author wishes to express his grateful appreciation to the following people for their contributions to the preservation and restoration of the Désert de Retz and for their efforts to perpetuate the memory of François Racine de Monville:

Dr. Pierre Morange

Mrs. Caroline Doucet

The late Jean-Louis Saury

Mr. Jean-Marc Heftler-Louiche

Mr. Dominique Césari

Mr. Laurent Fourquié

The author wishes to acknowledge a particular debt of gratitude to Mrs. Bénédicte Saury for her invaluable assistance in the preparation of this book.

Before the Désert de Retz

"View of a Hamlet from the Park named the Desert," by Constant Bourgeois (1767-1841), engraved by De Saulx and reproduced in *Le Nouveau Jardin Français* by Alexandre de Laborde, published in 1808.

Dans mon cœur agité, ramène l'espérance.
--François Racine de Monville

François Nicolas Henri Racine de Monville was the son of Jean-Baptiste Racine de Jonquoy (1694-1750),[4] a Receiver-General of Taxes, and Marie-Marthe-Françoise Le Monnier (1708-1742).

According to Monsieur de Monville's longtime acquaintance Jean-Nicolas Dufort de Cheverny (1731-1802), writing in his memoirs, Monville was born in 1733 near Alençon, in Normandy. However, an American author, Diana Ketcham, relying on contemporary records, writes in her well-researched book[5] that he was born on October 4, 1734, in Paris, in a building known as the Hôtel de Mesmes on the Rue Sainte-Avoie, now part of the Rue du Temple, in what is today the Third Arrondissement of Paris.

There appears to be a distant relationship between Monsieur de Monville's family and that of the dramatist Jean Racine (1639-1699). Monville's great-grandfather, Nicolas Racine (1617-1694), and Jean Racine's great-grandfather, were both natives of the town of Crépy-en-Valois.[6]

Monville's mother was the daughter of the wealthy Thomas Le Monnier (1677-1761), owner of a

---

[4] Also written "Joncquoy."

[5] *Le Désert de Retz: A Late Eighteenth-Century French Folly Garden – The Artful Landscape of Monsieur de Monville*, The MIT Press, 1997.

[6] For a more detailed discussion of Monville's ancestry, see the article by Claude and Denis Racine in Volume 11, Numéro 1, of *L'Enraciné*, a newsletter published by the Association des Familles Racine, in Sainte-Foy, Québec.

luxurious residence on the Rue Neuve des Petits-Champs in Paris and many estates in Normandy. The son of a draper in Elbeuf, Thomas Monnier had married one of his servants, Marie-Marthe-Francoise Martorey (? -1760), and received his charge through the good graces she had granted to the Duke of Luxembourg.

Until the French Revolution, people could modify their cognomens far more easily than is the case today. Thus, the man we generally refer to today as Monsieur de Monville went by a number of names during his lifetime. At birth, he was christened François Nicolas Henri Racine de Jonquoy. At his marriage on September 30, 1755, his maternal grandfather bestowed on him the Château du Thuit, near Les Andelys, in Normandy, and he replaced "de Jonquoy" with "du Thuit."[7] At the death of his maternal grandfather on July 6, 1761, he inherited the barony of Monville, and thereafter became known as the Baron de Monville.[8]

On June 19, 1790, titles of nobility were abolished in France and the use of family coats of arms was

---

[7] Monville sold the property in 1774 to René Nicolas de Maupéou (1714-1792), chancellor of France under Louis XV; Maupéou subsequently razed the château.

[8] Researchers should not confuse the subject of this book with the barons Alexandre Bigot de Monville (1607-1675), Thomas-Charles-Gaston Boissel de Monville (1763-1832) or Hippolyte Boissel de Monville (1794-1863).

prohibited, so Monville was no longer a baron. [9] Finally, after a law enacted on February 6, 1793, outlawed the use of any names other than those appearing on a person's birth certificate, he was referred to as "Citizen Racine known as Monville." The name on his death notice therefore reads "Racine, François Nicolas Henry [*sic*]."

According to some accounts, Monville spent his early childhood in the Château du Manais, in Ferrières-en-Bray, in Normandy, built in 1730. Today, the building is privately owned and not open to the public.

Thomas Le Monnier served as a *fermier général* or tax farmer from 1721 to 1761. Tax farming flourished in France after its founding in 1681 by Jean-Baptiste Colbert, and was essentially the privatization of tax collection by outsourcing the task to the Company of Farmers General, a chartered body that guaranteed the Crown a fixed sum of revenue in advance. Usually, the tax farmer deposited a lump sum to the public treasury; the difference between that sum and the amounts actually collected represented his profit or loss.

The *fermiers généraux* collected customs duties and taxes on alcohol and tobacco. The most hated and excessive of these imposts was known as the *gabelle*, a tax on salt, the sale of which had been a

---

[9] The de Jonquoy coat of arms is described as *Parti d'argent et de sinople à un lion rampant de l'un à l'autre.*

government monopoly since 1340. The main use of salt was not as a table seasoning, but as a preservative for meat to prevent microbial growth and putrefaction at a time when refrigeration was unknown. After being suspended in 1790 and reinstated by Napoleon Bonaparte in 1806, the *gabelle* was not abolished permanently until 1945.

It is no exaggeration to state that the *gabelle* was one of the principal causes of the French Revolution. From 1630 to 1710, the salt tax increased tenfold from 14 times the cost of production to 140 times the cost of production.

Just as the American Revolution began as a conflict over the legitimacy of British taxation in its American colonies, Eugene N. White, an American economist, noted that, "Inequitable and excessive taxation helped to incite the French Revolution... [T]he issue of taxation was a central part of the incendiary debates in the early days of the revolutionary upheaval. [The tax farmers] were depicted as rapacious and tyrannical." [10] Popular hatred soon developed against the huge profits of the tax farmers, and its organization was abolished in 1791.

Monville had only one sibling, an older sister named Marie-Henriette Racine de Jonquoy (1730-1791)

---

[10] White, Eugene N., *France's Slow Transition from Privatized to Government-Administered Tax Collection: Tax Farming in the Eighteenth Century*, Rutgers University, 2001.

who, by her marriage on March 2, 1745, to Jacques-Louis-Georges de Clermont d'Amboise (1726-1746), became the Marquise de Reynel.

In 1776, Marie-Henriette acquired the fifteenth-century Château de Chantereine in the town of Criel-sur-Mer on the coast of Normandy, which she transformed and to which annexed a chapel. She died on July 21, 1791, and her body was interred the following day. The château and grounds were confiscated by the revolutionary government, but subsequently returned to Marie-Henriette's heirs. The Château de Chantereine, as it was transformed by Monsieur de Monville's sister, is currently the property of the town of Criel-sur-Mer, and accommodates paying guests.

The daughter of Marie-Henriette and Jacques-Louis-Georges de Clermont d'Amboise, Thomasse-Thérèse de Clermont d'Amboise (1746-1789), was born just a month before her father died at the age of twenty. She married Jacques-Philippe de Choiseul-Stainville, on April 3, 1761. The couple had two daughters, Marie Stéphanie de Choiseul-Stainville (1763-1833) and Françoise-Thérèse Félicité de Choiseul-Stanville (1766-1794).

Marie Stéphanie married a cousin, Claude Antoine Gabriel de Choiseul-Stainville (1760-1838), with whom she had three children, two boys and a girl. In 1804 the eldest, Jacqueline Stéphanie de Choiseul-Stainville (1782-1861) married Philippe

Gabriel de Marmier (1763-1845), with whom she had three children.

Marie Stéphanie's son Antoine Clériadus de Choiseul-Stainville was born in 1783 and died in Vienna in 1809 leaving no progeny. René Auguste de Choiseul-Stanville was born in 1788 but appears to have died in infancy. Jacqueline and Antoine were two of Monsieur de Monville's four heirs, along with their aunt's two daughters.

Marie Stéphanie's sister Françoise-Thérèse married Joseph Marie Grimaldi, Prince of Monaco (1763-1816), thereby becoming Princess of Monaco. She followed her husband into exile during the Reign of Terror, entrusting her two young daughters, Princess Honorine Camille Grimaldi (1784-1879) and Princess Athénaïse Euphrasie Grimaldi (1786-1860), to her aunt Louise Honorine Crozat de Châtel, Duchess of Choiseul (1734-1801). Françoise-Thérèse missed her children and returned to France where she was arrested and, condemned to death. She wrote the prosecutor, the sinister Antoine Quentin Fouquier-Tinville (1746-1795), contesting the decision, arguing that she was a "foreign princess" condemned to death by "the injustice of French judges." Her appeal was to no avail: she was executed on July 27, 1794 (9 Thermidor II), at the age of twenty-seven. The niece of Monsieur de Monville addressed her last words to one of her companions in misfortune: "Be brave, my dear friend; crime alone displays weakness."

The body of Françoise-Thérèse was interred the day after her execution in one of the two mass graves located in the Picpus Cemetery in the Twelfth Arrondissement of Paris, where 1,109 men and 197 women were laid to rest, the 1,306 victims of the guillotine located on the nearby Place de la Barrière du Trône, first renamed Place du Trône Renversé and now known as the Place de la Nation.

Although it is commonly believed that execution by guillotine was reserved for aristocrats, the nobility and the clergy, in actual fact, half the male victims and 123 of the women were listed as *gens du people*—commoners. The Picpus Cemetery is open to the public and is of particular interest to Americans because it is the location of the tomb of the Marquis de Lafayette (1757-1834), over which an American flag waves eternally.

Had her execution been delayed by less than a day, Françoise-Thérèse would have survived, since Maximilien Robespierre (1758-1794), who was instrumental in condemning accused "enemies of the Revolution" to death, was executed himself late the next afternoon, along with his brother and 20 more of his partisans.

Robespierre, known to his supporters as "The Incorruptible," was born in the northern town of Arras. He and his three siblings were abandoned by their father shortly after their mother's death in 1764 and raised by their maternal grandmother and aunts.

Robespierre was a complex and enigmatic character who originally opposed the death penalty and advocated the abolition of slavery, but later defended the use of terror as the counterpart of virtue in a republic. [11] He never married but, according to various sources, he was engaged to Éléonore Duplay, the eldest daughter of has landlady; she wore widow's weeds after his death. Dr. Philippe Charlier, a medical examiner, determined that, based on contemporary accounts and a death mask, Robespierre not only displayed the prominent facial scars of smallpox but numerous symptoms of sarciodosis including vision problems, nosebleed, jaundice and asthenia. [12]

A law enacted on June 10, 1794, permitted honest citizens to be summarily executed merely because someone such an envious neighbor denounced them as counter-revolutionaries.

A discussion of the guillotine is appropriate at this juncture since it figures prominently in the pages that follow. Its sinister shadow loomed over many men and women from all walks of life, all ages and all strata of society, even threatening foreigners, at least one whom was an American citizen. Some

---

[11] The Société des études robespierristes, whose mission is to research and publish documents relating to Robespierre and his times, was founded in 1908; since 1936, a station on the Paris Metro, in the eastern suburb of Montreuil has borne the name "Robespierre."

[12] "Robespierre: the oldest case of sarcoidosis?" in *The Lancet*, Volume 382, Issue 9910, December 21, 2013.

escaped thanks to their silence, exile or cunning; many others, less fortunate, were doomed.

The guillotine had its origins in Scotland in the 16th and 17th centuries. Dr. Joseph-Ignace Guillotin (1738-1814), a Freemason and parliamentarian, advocated the adoption of the device as a humane method of administering capital punishment in contrast to the barbarous methods dating from the Middle Ages, including hanging, burning at the stake, the breaking wheel and decapitation with an axe, currently used in pre-revolutionary France.

One notorious example is the gruesome public execution of Robert-François Damiens (1715-1757), the last person in France to be drawn and quartered. Damiens was a mentally-deranged domestic servant who had attempted regicide by stabbing Louis XV with a small penknife at Versailles on January 5, 1757. Historian Laurence L. Bongie provides an account of Damien's excruciating death:

> "On the day of his execution, his offending hand was burned with sulfur. Pieces of flesh were then torn from his body with pincers, after which a mixture of molten lead and boiling pitch was ladled into the wounds...[T]he victim then watched as, first four, then six lurching horses harnessed to his four limbs proceeded to tear his legs and arms from his body."[13]

---

[13] Bongie, Laurence L., *From Rogue to Everyman: A Foundling's Journey to the Bastille*, Montreal, McGill-Queen's University Press, 2004.

Dr. Guillotin was appointed to a committee formed in 1791 to research a new method of capital punishment to be used on all condemned people regardless of class. Their deliberations were motivated by the very progressive notion that the purpose of capital punishment was strictly to end life rather than to inflict pain. The guillotine itself was actually the proposal of the chairman of the committee, a military surgeon named Dr. Antoine Louis, hence its early nickname, *la louisette*.

For most of Monsieur de Monville's contemporaries, what was most heinous about the guillotine was not so much the machine itself but the fact that it took the lives of so many thousands of completely innocent men and women—some of whose destinies are recounted in these pages—sentenced to death by fanatic magistrates without the benefit of due process.[14] The guillotine was utilized in France until 1977, and the country officially abolished the death penalty in 1981.[15]

The date of Françoise-Thérèse's execution, July 27, 1794, corresponded to the ninth day of the month of Thermidor of Year II on the French Republican

---

[14] According to the records, the oldest victims were two 92-year old women of the nobility, Anne Marie Louise Catherine Parisot and Marie Anne Josephine Douay. The youngest victims were 17 years old.

[15] For the record, a decision of the United States Supreme Court in the case of *Furman v. Georgia* in 1972 resulted in a moratorium on capital punishment. In 1976, however, in the case of *Gregg v. Georgia*, the august jurists voted 7 to 2 to end the *de facto* moratorium. As of 2015, capital punishment was legal in 31 of the 50 United States.

calendar, created by a politician and mathematician named Gilbert Romme (1750-1795) and intended by the revolutionary government to replace the Gregorian calendar.

The year was now divided into twelve months of thirty days each. Whereas most of the months of the old calendar were dedicated to Roman gods, the nomenclature of the Republican Calendar was invented by the poet and playwright Philippe Fabre d'Eglantine (1750-1794) and inspired by agricultural activities and climatic conditions. Born in Carcassonne, Philippe Fabre won a silver eglantine rose as a prize in the Floral Games in Toulouse and thenceforth added the attribute to his name. The Floral Games are conducted by the Académie des Jeux Floraux. Founded in 1373, it is the oldest literary institution in Europe and is still in existence.[16]

Although officially implemented on October 5, 1793, the first date on the calendar was fixed retroactively to September 22, 1792, the date of the proclamation of the First French Republic. This was also the date of the autumnal equinox, and it became the first day of Vendémiaire (Grape Harvest). The subsequent autumn months were Brumaire (Fog) and Frimaire (Frost), followed by the winter months of Nivôse

---

[16] Sentenced to death for forgery, Fabre handed out handwritten copies of his poems to onlookers on his way to the guillotine on April 5, 1794 (16 Germinal II).

(Snow) and Pluviôse (Rain) Ventôse (Wind), the spring months of Germinal (Germination), Floréal (Flowering), Prairial (Pasturing) and the summer months of Messidor (Harvest), Thermidor (Heat) and Fructidor (Fruit). The five or six additional days, known as *Sans-culottides*, [17] were national holidays, celebrated in autumn. The names of the saints associated with each day on the old calendar were replaced with those of animals, tools, plants and minerals.

The calendar was used for about 12 years, from late 1793 to 1805, and for 18 days by the Paris Commune in 1871. One of the principal reasons the calendar was abandoned was the abolition of the seven-day week. Instead, each month was divided into three ten-day weeks known as *décades*, whose days were named *Primidi, Duodi, Tridi, Quartidi, Quintidi, Sextidi, Septidi, Octidi, Nonidi and Décadi.*

Obviously, nobody wanted to give up a day of rest every seven days for one every ten days; some workers went on strike while others cleverly decided to work neither on Sunday on the old calendar nor Décadi on the new one, thus enjoying as many as seven days off per month. [18]

---

[17] Jour de la Vertu, Jour du Génie, Jour du Travail, Jour de l'Opinion, Jour des Récompenses and—on leap years—Jour de la Révolution.

[18] Romme was subsequently accused of supporting an insurrection and sentenced to death. Preferring suicide to the guillotine, he stabbed himself to death on June 17, 1795, 29 Prairial III on the calendar he created.

In 1793, France annexed the Principality of Monaco and confiscated the property of the Grimaldis, whose palace was converted into a hospice. Prince Joseph, declared enemy of the Revolution, fled across the Channel. Monaco was renamed Fort Hercule and incorporated into the *Département*[19] of Alpes-Maritimes. Prince Joseph returned to France at the end of 1795. Widowed, he married an Irish woman, Frances Rainford, and died in 1816. Fort Hercule remained French until 1814, when France retroceded part of the territory to the Grimaldis. Until 1847 the Principality of Monaco occupied a total area of 24 square kilometers incorporating three towns: Monaco, Menton and Roquebrune. Today, the principality only occupies an area of 202 hectares.

In March of 1742, Monsieur de Monville's father was convicted of fraud and jailed, [20] and on December 4, 1742, Monville's mother died, from chagrin, perhaps, or a broken heart. With his father incarcerated[21] and his mother deceased, the eight-year old Monville was placed under the guardianship of his wealthy maternal grandfather Thomas Le Monnier, who possessed sufficient

---

[19] In 1790, France was divided into 83 geographical entities, known as *départements*. The system has remained: as of 2011 there were 101 *départements,* 96 in continental Europe, the others overseas.

[20] Whatever his misdeeds, Jean-Baptiste Racine de Jonquoy was also an art-lover; a painting he owned, *Rendez-vous de Chasse* by Watteau, now hangs in the Wallace Collection in London.

[21] Jean-Baptiste Racine de Jonquoy died in the prison of Port-Louis, near Lorient, in 1750.

means to provide the youngster with a good education and upbringing, doubtlessly provided by private tutors, as was customary among the wealthy.

In the 1750's, Monsieur de Monville was still living in Paris with his grandfather on the Rue-Neuve-des-Petits-Champs, today the Rue des Petits-Champs. Monville's contemporary, Dufort de Cheverny, draws this portrait of Monville. He was "One of the most handsome eligible bachelors in Paris. He was 5 feet 8 inches tall[22] and looked like a god...his torso and legs would have made Antinoüs [23] envious...his head was a bit too small, but still attractive."

Dufort de Cheverny related in his memoirs that, late one night, Monville and some of his bachelor friends—Chabanon, La Borde and Fontanieu-Villecourt—as well as Dufort himself, most likely after having imbibed copious quantities of wine, decided to serenade a certain Madame Brissard, who was La Borde's sister and the wife of a tax farmer, underneath her window in the Hôtel Bullion.[24] The lady, awakened, appeared at her window holding what Monville and his friends took to be her nightcap, which they expected she would toss down

---

[22] The French used feet and inches until December 20, 1799, when the metric system was officially adopted.

[23] Antinoüs (111-130 AD) was a favorite of the Roman emperor Hadrian and was deified after his death,

[24] The Hôtel Bullion was built in 1630. The central Paris post office, on the Rue du Louvre, occupies the site today.

to them as a trophy. Unfortunately, it was a chamber pot. Undaunted, the swains decided to serenade the actress Astraudi and were pursued by the night watchmen. Dufort bought three of them home but neglected Fontanieu, who was apprehended, but ended up as the guest at the police commissioner's home, where he ate, drank and made merry until four in the morning!

To gain an idea of Monville's youthful companions, Pierre-Elisabeth de Fontanieu-Villecourt (1730-1784) became the Commissary General and Comptroller of the French crown's furniture. Michel Paul Guy de Chabanon (1730-1792), a virtuoso violinist, would be named to the Académie Française in 1779. Jean-Benjamin de La Borde (1734-1794), a tax farmer, was a prolific, albeit mediocre, composer. Incarcerated in the same prison as Monville, he would die on the guillotine.

According to Dufort de Cheverny, Monville danced so well that he was invited to all the balls. He was an accomplished horseman, excelled at *le jeu de paume*, known today as real tennis in Great Britain and court tennis in America. He could shoot a bow-and-arrow "as well as an Indian." He played the flute "like Amphion."

It is during this period that Monville, considered a musical prodigy, traveled to Berlin where he was introduced to King Frederick II of Prussia (1712-1786), and performed on the flute in a number of concerts at Frederick the Great's Sanssouci palace in Potsdam. Frederick was, like Monville, a talented flautist and composed a hundred sonatas for flute and four symphonies. His court musicians included Johann Joachim Quantz and Carl Philipp Emanuel Bach.

Armandine Rolland (1769-1852),[25] writing in *La Famille Sainte-Amaranthe*, published in 1864, reports that Frederick the Great was so impressed with Monville's ability to execute some difficult passages, that he exclaimed, "This young Frenchman is an Apollo!" Her emembrances of Monville are so detailed that they warrant citing *in extenso*.

> I remember Monsieur de Monville who, in those days, combined the glamour of beauty, great wealth and a rare talent as a musician. He created the delicious Désert in the Forêt de Marly where he hosted wonderful parties. In Monville's youth, tourism didn't exist as it does now: only great lords and wealthy financiers were able to roam the capitals of Europe, and Monville was not left behind...The days of parties ended in 1791, as youth, possessions and wealth existed no more. The flute was broken and the Désert sold. But Monville remained a man of kindness and fashion, conversing pleasantly about any subject, even gastronomy, where he would have been a worthy rival of Brillat-Savarin.

It is not difficult to understand why Frederick the Great would have welcomed Monville to his court. Having mastered French in his youth, Frederick

---

[25] Born Josephine-Armande (Lucile) Marchandeau de l'Isle and divorced in 1792 from Sieur de Barréron (or Barrairon), she knew Monville personally and delivered a first-hand, detailed and moving account of Madame de Sainte-Amaranthe's salon and the fate of her family.

34

developed an early interest in that country's culture and philosophy and invited Voltaire (1694-1778) to live at Sanssouci in 1750. Both Frederick and Monville commissioned buildings from the neoclassical and visionary architect Etienne-Louis Boullée (1728-1799). [26] And, whether or not Monville was a Freemason, Frederick definitely was, having joined a lodge in 1738.

Monville took harp lessons along with his fellow student and lifelong friend, Pierre-Augustin Caron de Beaumarchais, from a German teacher known as Gaiffre l'Ainé,[27] and nicknamed "King David."

As a token of his friendship, Beaumarchais penned a 52-line, rhymed *Epitre à mon Ami* dedicated to Monville. This epistle showers high praise on Monville for his many talents and accomplishments, even suggesting that he could be a professor. But he also gently chides his friend for courting so many women and recommends that Monville "love but one." The manuscript of this heretofore unpublished document is in the Bibliothèque Nationale de France; the poem itself is reproduced in the Appendix.

Monville became so proficient on the harp that he accompanied his favorite composer, Christoph Willibald Gluck (1714-1787), and, in the mid-

---

[26] Boullée's grandiose yet unrealized designs are astonishing in their scope, and his vision has remained influential, as in Wallace K. Harrison's Perisphere, the symbol, along with the Trylon, of the 1939 World's Fair in New York.

[27] His real name was Georges-Adam Goepfert (c. 1727-1809). He introduced the single-action pedal harp to Paris in 1749.

1750's, he would be invited to perform with Madame de Genlis during her twice-weekly salons.

Beaumarchais, like Monville, was one of the most complex and enigmatic personalities to emerge in the French Enlightenment. Although he is most recognized today as a playwright, the author of *Le Mariage de Figaro, Le Barbier de Séville* and *La Mère coupable*, the first two adapted into operas, Beaumarchais was, in his day, equally noteworthy as an inventor, diplomat, secret agent, publisher and financier.

Born Pierre-Augustin Caron in Paris on January 24, 1732, into a family of Huguenot watchmakers originating in the town of Lizy-sur-Ourcq, northeast of Paris, he followed the family trade and invented the double virgule escapement mechanism for small portable watches before the age of twenty. Another of his early accomplishments was a rectangular watch mounted on a ring, made for Madame de Pompadour in 1755. This elegant and unique *montre-bague* was wound by turning the bezel, and the time set with a tiny key.

Shortly after his marriage to Madeleine-Catherine Aubertin[28] on November 22, 1756, Monsieur Caron became "Caron de Beaumarchais," adding a name he had derived from "le Bois Marchais," a woodland

---

[28] Madeleine-Catherine Aubertin and Beaumarchais's second wife, Geneviève-Madeleine Lévêque, were wealthy widows. Both died under mysterious circumstances.

belonging to his wife. Less than a year later, his wife succumbed, reportedly, to typhoid fever. His second wife, Geneviève-Madeleine Wettebled Lévêque, another widow, died after a short marriage to Beaumarchais bequeathing a large fortune to him. In both cases, rumors circulated that these wealthy women did not die of natural causes. In 1786 Beaumarchais married his third wife, Marie-Thérèse Willermanulas (1751-1816), from Canton Fribourg in Switzerland, who gave him a daughter.

Beaumarchais not only expressed his revolutionary sentiments in France; he was among the early French supporters of American independence from Great Britain, writing in a brochure, "The cause of America is in many ways the cause of humanity."

Beaumarchais was known at the court in Versailles because of his previous activities—he had given harp lessons to Louis XV's four daughters and become a musical advisor to the royal family—and for his services as an undercover agent in London, where he prevented the publication of a pamphlet denouncing Madame du Barry and purchased incriminating documents in the possession of the Chevalier d'Eon, a notorious cross-dressing French diplomat and fencer.

Beaumarchais lobbied the French government on behalf of the American insurgents and played a pivotal role in convincing Louis XVI to provide them with weapons, munitions, uniforms and provisions in the years before France's formal entry into the war for American independence in 1778.

In 1751, Monville competed with Dufort de Cheverny for the post of Introducer of Ambassadors at the court of Louis XV. Monville lost the competition, his candidacy possibly harmed by his late father's conviction and imprisonment for fraud. Nevertheless, Monville and Dufort remained acquaintances thereafter, and both survived the Reign of Terror.

Dufort de Cheverny was born on February 3, 1731, into a family of parliamentarians and tax farmers. He was fifteen when his father died, bequeathing him a considerable fortune that he dissipated on amusements and entertainment. After serving as Introducer of Ambassadors, he retired from the court in 1764. The next year, he undertook a substantial renovation of the château of Cheverny and laid out a park on its grounds.

Dufort de Cheverny was arrested in May 1794 and imprisoned at Blois, where he began to write his memoirs. The end of the Reign of Terror left him free but ruined due to the depreciation of his investments. He died on February 28, 1802, at the age of 71. His *Memoirs of the Reign of Louis XV and Louis XVI and the French Revolution*[29] would be published in 1886.

On September 30, 1755, Monsieur de Monville married his third cousin, Aimable Charles Félicité Lucas de Boncourt. The marriage was short-lived and produced no progeny. Monville was widowed in December 1760.

In 1756, thanks to the contacts and the generosity of his grandfather, Monsieur de Monville paid 630,000 *livres* to acquire the post of Grand Master of Waters and Forests of Normandy in Rouen, a position he would hold until he relinquished it to Louis-Joseph de Mondran in 1763. Sustainable forestry has a long history in France, dating as far back as the 13th century. Royal forests were managed in order to produce income from the sale of lumber and assure stewardship over wildlife and game. Each region of France had its own Master of Waters and Forests. During his tenure, Monville developed a passionate interest in botany, agronomy and horticulture and took his job seriously.

Jean-Claude Waquet cites a letter by Monville written on December 28, 1757, recommending reforesting with pine the areas in the Forêt de Rouvray where beech had not been successful and

---

[29] Dufort's memoirs may be consulted on Gallica.fr, the website of the Bibliothèque Nationale de France. Facsimile reprints are also available.

estimated that, when mature, the trees could generate an annual income of 40,000 *livres.*[30]

In 1761, the Austrian landscape painter and engraver Franz Edmund Weirotter (1733-1771) produced a suite of six etchings depicting scenes in the environs of the town of Les Andelys, not far from the Château du Thuit, which Monville owned at the time. The dedication reads: "To Monsieur de Monville, Grand Master of Waters and Forests, by his very humble and very obedient servant, F.E. Weirotter."

When Monville's grandfather, Thomas Le Monnier, died in 1761, he bequeathed his grandson a considerable inheritance, estimated at over 4,000,000 *livres.* About this time, Monville made the acquaintance of Stéphanie Félicité Ducrest de Saint-Aubin. In her memoirs, she described Monville as "A magnificent suitor—a young widower, rich and handsome—as if he had stepped out of the pages of a novel." But, alas, "He did not have a place in the court [i.e. at Versailles."

Monville's proposal of marriage in 1761 was declined. The following year, Stéphanie married Charles-Alexis Brûlart de Genlis, a colonel of the

---

[30] Waquet, Jean-Claude, *Les Grands maîtres des eaux et forêts de France de 1689 à la Révolution,* Genève, Droz, 1978.

grenadiers, with whom she had three children. During the Reign of Terror, he was condemned to death on the guillotine and executed on October 31, 1793 (10 Brumaire II).

During her lifetime, Madame de Genlis became a noted writer, musician and educator, pioneering and anticipating a number of modern teaching methods: she taught history with the aid of magic lantern slides and engaged a botanist to lead her students on pedagogical nature walks.

In 1781, Madame de Genlis was appointed as governess of the daughters of the cousin of Louis XVI, Louis Philippe Joseph, Duc d'Orléans (1747-1793).[31]

Madame de Genlis was also the presumed mother of an illegitimate daughter named Pamela after the eponymous heroine of Samuel Richardson's epistolary novel, published in 1740 and the fruit of her liaison with the Duc d'Orléans. The girl was legally adopted by Madame de Genlis and her husband and became Pamela Brûlart de Sillery (c. 1777-1830). During a voyage to Paris in October 1792, an Irish aristocrat, Lord Edward FitzGerald (1763-1798), who was lodging as the guest of the American patriot and philosopher Thomas Paine (1737-1809), espied Pamela at the theater and was

---

[31] He was known as the Duc de Chartres from 1752 to 1785, when he succeeded his father as Duc d'Orléans. He referred to himself as Philippe-Egalité from 1792 until his death in 1793.

introduced to her. The two were married on December 27, 1792.[32] Rendered penniless after the unexpected death of her husband in 1798, Pamela fled to Hamburg to escape her creditors, where she briefly encountered her presumed mother. She died in poverty in Paris on December 31, 1830.

In 1789 Madame de Genlis had shown herself favorable to the French Revolution, but events in 1793 compelled her to take refuge in Switzerland. Her ten-volume *Mémoires inédits sur le XVIIIᵉ siècle et la Révolution françoise* were published starting in 1825, and she died on December 31, 1830.

In 1762, the year after his rejection by Stéphanie de Genlis, Monville met the 18-year old Jeanne Bécu, who would subsequently receive the title of Comtesse du Barry as the *maîtresse-en-titre* of Louis XV. Jeanne was born in 1743, the illegitimate daughter of Anne Bécu, who left her native Lorraine to seek her fortune in Paris, taking Jeanne, then age three, with her. When Jeanne was six, her mother placed her in the Convent of Saint Aure, where she remained until she was fifteen. Upon leaving the convent, Jeanne eventually found work as a milliner's assistant in a haberdashery named À la Toilette, owned by Marie-Anne Saint-Martin and operated by her husband, Claude-Edmé Labille. Jeanne's beauty was so exceptional that Monville is

---

[32] She was named for the eponymous heroine of Samuel Richardson's epistolary novel, published in 1740. After the death of FitzGerald, in 1789, she emigrated to Hamburg, where she was briefly reunited with her putative mother. She died in squalor in Paris in 1831.

reported to have told his friends that artists would approach her and beg to paint her in the nude.

Jeanne befriended the Labille's daughter, Adélaïde Labille-Guiard (1749-1803), who became an acclaimed portraitist and miniaturist, inducted on May 31, 1783, into the French *Académie Royale de Peinture et de Sculpture* along with Elisabeth-Louise Vigée Le Brun (1755-1842), praised for her portraits of the French royal family and other worthies.

Jeanne also attracted the attention of Jean-Baptiste du Barry (1723-1794); a high-class procurer nicknamed *Le Roué*, who owned a casino. Du Barry installed her in his household and made her his mistress. Giving her the sobriquet "Mademoiselle Lange"—the Angel—du Barry helped establish Jeanne's career as a courtesan in the upper echelons of Parisian society; this enabled her to acquire several aristocratic men, including Monville, as brief lovers or clients. Monville, who showed steadfast loyalty to his friends, maintained his intimate friendship with Madame du Barry throughout his life.

After her expulsion from the court at the death of her protector Louis XV, she retired to her pavilion, designed by Claude-Nicolas Ledoux (1736-1806), in the town of Louveciennes, only ten kilometers from Chambourcy. She and Monville would frequently visit each other until her arrest and imprisonment on

September 22, 1793 (1 Vendémiaire II). She was put to death on December 8, 1793 (18 Frimaire II).[33]

In addition to the future Madame du Barry, during the first half of the 1760's, Monsieur de Monville was observed to have enjoyed the company of a number of *femmes galantes*, including Anne Thoynard de Jouy, Comtesse d'Esparbès, a former favorite of Louis XV; actresses such as "the charming Rosalie Astraudy from the Comédie Italienne" and opera singers, notably Sophie Arnould, Anne Demerville de Saint-Rémy, known as Madame de Saint-Janvier, and many others!

After the death of Madame de Pompadour, Madame d'Esparbès (1739-1825) expected to become the successor to her late cousin, but the honor fell instead on Béatrix de Choiseul-Stainville, duchesse de Gramont, the sister-in-law of Monville's niece, Thomasse-Thérèse Clermont d'Amboise.

The saucy Madame d'Esparbès figured in a number of amusing anecdotes. On one occasion she and some friends were invited to "admire the male anatomy" in the atelier of the sculptor Edmé Bouchardon (1709-1762). To protect the modesty of his female visitors, he had affixed fig leaves in

---

[33] Unlike most of the victims of the guillotine, who met their fates stoically or—like Monville—awaited their fate with nonchalance or resignation, Charles-Henri Sanson (1739-1806), the High Executioner, describes in his memoirs the heart-rending spectacle of Madame du Barry hysterically proclaiming her innocence and pleading for mercy. Jean-Baptiste du Barry also ended his days on the guillotine, in Toulouse.

appropriate locations. All of the ladies waxed enthusiastic over these gods of Antiquity save Madame d'Esparbès, who observed that she could not venture an opinion on them until the autumn, after the leaves had fallen.

Monsieur de Monville figures in another account. In a conversation, Louis XV observed to Madame d'Esparbès, "You have slept with all my subjects." "Ah, sire!" "You bedded the Duke of Choiseul." "He is so powerful." "The Duc de Richelieu."[34] "He is so lively." "Monville." "His legs are so shapely." "That may be so, but what about the Duc d'Aumont, who has none of those qualities?" "Ah, Sire, he is so devoted to Your Majesty!" After being forced into exile near Montauban, she wrote an epistle in verse in 1779 that won a prize in the Floral Games in Toulouse.

Rosalie Astraudy had bestowed her charms on a number of wealthy protectors, most of them tax farmers, as well as Charles-Guillaume Le Normant d'Étiolles (1717-1799), the husband of Madame de Pompadour ridiculed as the most famous cuckold in France. She was also the mother of the illegitimate child of Guy-Félix Pignatelli, Comte d'Egmont, who had battered her when he found her in bed with the Marquis de Monac. Egmont was fatally injured in a duel and died at the age of 32 on July 3, 1753.

---

[34] Louis François Armand de Vignerot du Plessis de Richelieu (1696-1788)

Sophie Arnould (1740-1802) was considered the greatest soprano of her day. She starred as Eurydice in Gluck's opera *Orphée et Eurydice* and in the title role in *Iphigénie en Aulide* and obtained considerable success in works by the virtuoso violinist François Francœur (1698-1787), Jean-Philippe Rameau (1683-1764) and Pierre-Alexandre Monsigny (1729-1817), one of the originators of the genre known as *opéra comique*.

According to Sophie Arnould's contemporaries, her voice was more beautiful than powerful, but she was a passionate actress. She was much in demand in Parisian society, and legend has it that Madame de Pompadour her "With such talents, you could become a princess." In point of fact, Sophie Arnould eventually became a mistress of the writer Louis-Léon-Félicité de Brancas (1733-1824), with whom she had four children.

Sophie Arnould was a *salonnière*—or salonist—one of those brilliant and cultivated Frenchwomen who hosted salons, literary and artistic functions attracting artists, musicians, philosophers and celebrities of their day. The *salonnières* inspired their guests to engage in educated, amusing and enlightening conversation, and the gatherings were frequently accompanied by music. The salon movement reached its apogee in the 18th century.

Sophie Arnould's guests included the philosopher Voltaire and his friend and fellow Freemason

Benjamin Franklin, the chronicler Louis Petit de Bachaumont, and Monville's friends Beaumarchais, Gluck and the poet Claude Joseph Dorat. She received twice a week; Thursdays were reserved exclusively for women. Sophie Arnould survived the Reign of Terror and died in 1802, penurious and forgotten, leaving her *Souvenirs* and an abundant correspondence.

At a time when society was defined and regulated almost completely by men, the *salonnières* played an important role in the social, political and cultural life of the French Enlightenment. Approximately twenty-five salons in Paris during the 18th century were hosted by women, and Monsieur de Monville was acquainted with other salonists aside from Sophie Arnould.

Both Monville and Dufort de Cheverny were the guests of the writer Louise d'Epinay, who gathered brilliant men of letters and philosophers, first at her château in Montmorency and, after 1770, in her home in Paris. Madame d'Epinay had been friendly with the political philosopher Jean-Jacques Rousseau (1712-1778), but after he criticized her indirectly in his *Confessions*, she responded in kind with her *Contre-Confessions*.[35]

Monsieur de Monville is also known to have attended the salon of the widow Anne-Catherine de

---

[35] The work—with the names changed—was published under the title *Histoire de Madame de Montbrillant* in 1818.

Ligniville, Madame Helvétius (1722-1800). She hosted her salon in her home at 59, Rue d'Auteuil, and for over five decades attracted the most eminent personalities of the Enlightenment. Her guests included Thomas Jefferson and Olympe de Gouges, author of the *Declaration of the Rights of Woman and the Female Citizen.*

Olympe de Gouges (1748-1793) was born Marie Gouze, the daughter of a butcher, in Montauban. Married in 1765, her husband Louis Aubry died the following year. In 1770 she relocated to Paris with her son Pierre, adopted an aristocratic-sounding name (she was convinced that her godfather, the Marquis Jean Jacques Le Franc de Pompignan (1709-1784), a poet and playwright, was her biological father) and became a prolific woman of letters, supported financially by her wealthy male acquaintances. Her efforts on behalf of gender equality and her publications denouncing the excesses of the Revolution were rewarded with a trip to the guillotine, where she was executed on November 3, 1793 (13 Brumaire II).[36]

One can only imagine the exchange of views that might have taken place between Jefferson, the author of the American Declaration of Independence,

---

[36] After his mother's death, Pierre Aubry de Gouges left France for French Guyana with his family. His daughter Marie Hyacinthe Geneviève married an English officer, William Wood; his other daughter, Charlotte, married Congressman Robert S. Garnett of Virginia. Consequently, Olympe de Gouges has many descendants in England and America.

and the French feminist and wonder whether Monsieur de Monville shared her views on the equality of the sexes.

Benjamin Franklin also regularly attended Madame Helvétius's salon. He grew fond of her, sanctified her "Notre Dame d'Auteuil" and proposed marriage. Even though the proposal was declined, Madame Helvétius was probably overjoyed to have a suitor as devoted and accomplished as Benjamin Franklin. Although her late husband, a wealthy tax farmer named Claude-Adrien Helvétius (1715-1771) was known publicly as a philosopher and poet, in his private hours his favorite recreation was anything but intellectual: the great thinker enjoyed being flagellated by dominatrix prostitutes, who were rewarded with a *louis d'or* for their services. A police report cited by Professor Bongie documents one session with a Mademoiselle Julie, who administered such a vigorous thrashing with her scourge that she drew blood, then compelled Helvétius to beg for mercy on his knees.

In 1777, before meeting Madame Helvétius, Franklin, who lived close to Auteuil, in the adjacent village of Passy, had fallen in love with one of his neighbors, Anne Louise Boyvin d'Hardancourt Brillon de Jouy (1744-1824). In his *Autobiography*, in an entry dated April 10, 1778, John Adams (1735-1826) describes a dinner party at the Brillons' residence to which he and Franklin had been invited. Adams reported that Madame Brillon was "one of the most beautiful women in France" and described her as "all softness, sweetness and politeness." Considered one of the best harpsichord players in Europe, she composed music and performed on the newly-invented fortepiano.

Franklin was a widower, his common-law wife Deborah Read (1708-1774) having died two years previously; but Madame Brillon was married and the mother of two young daughters, Cunégonde, born in 1764, and Aldegonde, born c. 1768. For Adams, Jacques Brillon de Jouy (1720-1787)—twenty-four years older than his wife—was "a rough kind of country squire." Adams continued,

> I saw a Woman in Company, as a Companion of Madam Brillon who dined with her at Table, and was considered as one of the Family. She was very plain and clumzy. When I afterwards learned both from Dr. Franklin[37] and his Grandson, and from many other Persons, that this Woman was the Amie[38] of Mr. Brillion and that Madam Brillion consoled herself by the Amitie of Mr. Le Vailliant,[39] I was astonished that these People could live together in such apparent Friendship and indeed without cutting each other's throats.

In the spirit of medieval courtly love, however, the affair between Franklin and Madame Brillon

---

[37] In February 1759 the University of St. Andrews had awarded Franklin an Honorary Doctor of Laws degree.

[38] This "Amie" was Mademoiselle Jupin, the children's governess. She was subsequently expelled from the household.

[39] Adams is referring to Louis-Guillaume Le Veillard, the Brillons' neighbor.

appears to have remained chaste and literary: she sent him one hundred three missives; he replied with twenty-nine.

One of Franklin's epistles was a flirtatious love-letter in the form of a "Treaty of Peace," with nine articles. Article Four stated, "That when he is with her, he shall be oblig'd to drink Tea, play Chess, hear Musick; or do any other thing that she requires of him."[40] In another letter, Franklin proposed a marriage between Cunégonde (then age seventeen) and his grandson Temple (twenty-one), whom the Brillons had nicknamed Franklinet. Cunégonde's father opposed the marriage since Temple was not a Catholic; on October 23, 1783, she married Colonel Antoine-Marie Paris d'Illins.

Temple later turned his affection to Aldegonde, and his feelings were reciprocated. This time, the match appeared to meet with the approval of Aldegonde's parents but, too late: following the example of his father and his grandfather, "Franklinet" had sired an illegitimate son. Blanchette Callot, a married woman, gave birth to Theodore Joseph Franklin (Callot) on February 22, 1785. The infant died in 1787.[41]

We may be surprised to discover three generations of Franklins who had sired illegitimate children. However, during the 18th century, such practices were common and, in countries such as England and

---

[40] The full text is reproduced in Franklin's *Autobiography*.

[41] See Lopez, Claude-Anne, *Mon Cher Papa: Franklin and the Ladies of Paris*, Yale University Press, 1990.

France, most of these newborns were taken by their mothers or, anonymously, by the midwives who had brought them into the world, to foundling hospices, where they were legally abandoned. Statistics compiled by the natural historian Georges-Louis Leclerc, Comte de Buffon, and cited by Professor Bongie, reveal that in 1756, 3,283 infants were taken to the Hospice des Enfants Trouvés in Paris and that the number increased to 7,676 in 1772, representing a startling 41% of all the live births in the city that year. The philosopher Rousseau quite candidly defended the serial abandonment of five of his illegitimate offspring in Book Seven of his *Confessions*. Many of the foundlings died in their infancy; those who survived were placed with honest, working-class families. Given the morays of the day and the fact that Monsieur de Monville frequented female denizens of the *demi-monde*, it is not inconceivable that among the many thousands of foundlings may have been offspring he begot.

Another salon that Monville frequented was nicknamed the "antechamber of the Académie Française," and was hosted by Élisabeth-Josèphe de Laborde, Comtesse d'Angivillers (1725-1798). Julien Cendres and Chloé Radiguet report[42] that her soirées were attended by many members of that august body, including Marc-Antoine d'Argenson, Marquis de Paulmy (1722-1787); Jean Le Rond d'Alembert (1717-1783), co-editor of the *Encyclopédie*; Claude-Henri Watelet (1718-1786), a

---

[42] *Le Désert de Retz, paysage choisi*, Paris, Éditions de l'Éclat, 2009.

tax farmer who was a connoisseur of gardens and the author of *Essai sur les jardins*, published in 1774; the poet Jacques Delille (1738-1813), who had sojourned at the Désert de Retz; the aphorist Nicolas Chamfort (1740-1794); the dramatist Marie-Joseph Chénier (1764-1811) and the parliamentarian Philippe-Antoine Merlin de Douai (1754-1838).

There are yet other salons whose guests included Monville's friends and that he might also have frequented. Sophie de Condorcet (1764-1822), was a highly-educated writer, fluent in English and Italian. She hosted a multinational salon where not only Jefferson and Olympe de Gouges were habitués, but Beaumarchais, the Marquis de Lafayette (1757-1834) and Thomas Paine, whose works, along with those of the English political economist Adam Smith, she translated into French. One of the reasons that Jefferson and Paine would have found the ambiance so congenial is that Sophie and her husband, the Marquis Nicolas de Condorcet (1743-1794), a philosopher and mathematician, spoke English. Jefferson spoke passable French, but Paine none.

Many of Monville's friends and acquaintances, including the Duc d'Orléans; Jacques Delille; Madame de Genlis and Louis Carrogis, known as Carmontelle (1717-1806)—who painted the Désert de Retz—attended the salon of playwright Charlotte-Jeanne Béraud de La Haye de Riou,

Madame de Montesson (1738-1806), the morganatic wife of Louis Philippe I, Duc d'Orléans (1725-1785).

Guests to the salon of Suzanne Curchod—Madame Necker—included American envoys Benjamin Franklin and Gouverneur Morris (1752-1816). Madame Necker (1737-1794), born in the French-speaking Swiss canton of Vaud, was the daughter of a pastor. After an early romance with the English historian Edward Gibbon, she married the wealthy banker and fellow Protestant Jacques Necker (1732-1804), born in the then-Republic of Geneva,[43] who served as Louis XVI's finance minister until 1790. Their only child, Germaine, was the prominent salonist and woman of letters known as Madame de Staël, who was married to the Swedish ambassador, Erik Magnus Staël von Holstein. Instead of squandering her husband's money on baubles and frivolities like so many of her peers, Madame Necker founded and endowed the first pediatric hospital in the world in Paris 1794; it still bears her name.

And, in the irony of ironies, both Thomas Paine and Maximilien Robespierre attended the salon of Madame Roland, née Marie-Jeanne Phlippon (1754-1793); Paine was later arrested under Robespierre's orders and sentenced to death on the guillotine, but instead languished in prison for almost a year. The unfortunate Madame Roland met her death on the

---

[43] The Republic of Geneva was proclaimed in 1541 and joined the Helvetic Confederation in 1815 as the 22nd canton.

scaffold on November 8, 1793 (18 Brumaire II). Her famous last words were, "*O Liberté, que de crimes on commet en ton nom!*" [44]

After having rented a number of buildings in Paris, Monville—like Thomas Jefferson, whom he would befriend many years later, an amateur architect—drew up the plans for a permanent Paris residence. According to Luc-Vincent Thiéry,[45] the neoclassical Grand Hôtel de Monville was located 21, Rue d'Anjou and was accompanied by a smaller building at number 22 on the same street, known as the Petit Hôtel de Monville, most likely reserved for guests or staff. On June 6, 1764, Monville signed a contract with Etienne-Louis Boullée to execute the project, which was completed in 1766.

Total cost of the two structures was 111,949 *livres*. In 1726, the value of a *livre* was set at 0.312 grams of 24-carat gold; in 2013, the same amount of gold would be worth approximately €14.55 or $20.00. Thus, in 2013, the two buildings would have cost approximately €1,630,000 or $2,400,000. The table below shows the prices of some common staples.[46]

---

[44] Her husband, Jean Marie Roland, learning of her death two days later, committed suicide.

[45] Thiéry, Luc-Vincent, *Guide des amateurs et des étrangers voyageurs à Paris*, Tome Premier, Paris, Hardouin & Gattey, 1787.

[46] The prices in *livres* were recorded in a village in southwest France. The prices in euros were compiled in a Paris supermarket. In the 18th century, sugar and coffee were imported and thus extremely costly. Poultry and eggs were produced locally.

Product	Unit	Price in livres in 1781	Equivalent price in euros	Price in euros in 2013
Sugar	Pound	1.80	26.19	1.00
Coffee	Pound	1.20	17.46	6.50
Chicken	One	0.30	4.37	9.00
Duck	One	0.75	10.91	12.00
Eggs	Dozen	0.25	3.63	2.00
Apples	Pound	0.75	10.91	1.50

Contemporary accounts describe the interior of the Grand Hôtel de Monville with awe and admiration. According to Thiéry, one room was designed as an "Asiatic pavilion with vistas of trees and female nudes holding draperies." In a letter dated July 26, 1776,[47] an anonymous visitor remarked that all the rooms on the ground floor contained "a prodigious quantity of clocks in bizarre shapes."

Monville's Turkish salon, decorated with mirrors, illustrated the French fascination with the Ottoman Empire dating from the beginning of the 18th century. Several operas and plays with Turkish themes were performed in 1776 and 1777 at the French court, enhancing the nobility's interest in the Turkish style, and launching a taste for interiors à la turque or "in the Turkish style." It would appear that Monville's Turkish salon, dating from 1766, was a precursor, since Marie Antoinette's recently restored *boudoir turque* at Fontainebleau dates originally from 1777.

---

[47] The letter is one of six, archived in the Bibliothèque Nationale de France.

According to historian Charles Leroux-Cesbron, in an essay published in 1914 entitled *M. de Monville: l'éternel ennuyé*, the centerpiece of the music room was a harpsichord "decorated by Rubens" which cost 10,000 livres, inscribed with a text in Latin, *Me fecit Antverpiæ anno 1637*. The instrument was the product of the Antwerp harpsichord-maker Johannes Ruckers (1578-1642) and was sold with all the other furniture after Monville's properties were acquired by Lewis Disney-Ffytche in 1792.[48] Described as a "beautiful harpsichord," it was registered in the inventory of 367 musical instruments confiscated during the Reign of Terror prepared by Antonio-Bartoloméo Bruni, a violinist at the Comédie Italienne. The document is conserved in the French National Archives and was published in 1890 with an introduction by J. Gallay.

The Ruckers family contributed immensely to the technical development of the harpsichord and the quality of their instruments is such that the name of Ruckers is as important for keyboard instruments as the Stradivarius is for the violin family. The Antwerp painters, including Rubens, received commissions to decorate the lids and casings of these harpsichords, which not only produced music but were pleasing to the eye. About 35 harpsichords built by Johannes Ruckers exist today, perhaps that of Monville among them.

---

[48] The furniture in the two buildings was sold for 25,245 livres on 12 Ventôse II (March 2, 1793).

Monville also equipped his townhouse with an original central heating system, consisting of a series of stoves connected by pipes concealed in the walls, and ending in radiators called *calorifères*, reportedly the first such installation built in France since the times of the Romans, over 1,500 years previously. His dinner parties hosted in the sumptuously-decorated townhouse might be accompanied by as many as seven continuous hours of music, including compositions by Monsigny, Rameau and Mozart,[49] performed by his consort of six musicians from their gallery.

Dufort de Cheverny's memoirs provide a vivid description of "a delightful evening" as Monville's guest. The rooms were lit "as bright as day," and the bedroom reminded him of something out of the Arabian Nights.

Monville's guests that evening included Sophie Arnould, Jean-Philippe de Franquetot de Coigny, who would marry the widow of Monville's friend Denis Thiroux de Montsauge in 1796, and a Francophile Irish nobleman, "Lord Powerscourt," who had impressed Parisians in October 1754 by wagering 1,500 *louis d'or* that he could ride from Fontainebleau to Paris in under two hours, winning his bet with nearly half an hour to spare, sacrificing

---

[49] Wolfgang Amadeus Mozart (1756-1791) visited in Paris on three occasions: November 1763 to April 1764, May to July 1766 and March to September 1778. During part of August 1778, Mozart resided at the Hôtel de Noailles in Saint-Germain-en-Laye, not far from the Désert de Retz.

two of his prize English thoroughbreds in the process. [50]

Another frequent guest at the banquets in the Grand Hôtel de Monville was the soldier and diplomat Etienne François de Choiseul (1719-1785). Monville's niece, Thomasse-Thérèse de Clermont d'Amboise (1746-1789), had married Choiseul's brother, Jacques-Philippe de Choiseul-Stainville, on April 3, 1761.

During the eighteenth century, Europeans coveted Chinese imports and developed an intense interest in Chinese clothes, porcelain, tea, and other items. Both Choiseul and Monville shared a love of *chinoiserie*, the term coined by the French to express this fascination with all things Chinese.

In 1770, for a number of reasons, including a diplomatic crisis over the Falkland Islands [51] between Britain and Spain,[52] Choiseul, then minister

---

[50] Dufort de Cheverny appears to be mistaken here. Professor Bongie writes that Edward Wingfield, 2nd Viscount Powerscourt, nicknamed "Milord Trousse-Cotte," because of his proclivity for lifting women's skirts, was the rider in the Fontainbleau-to-Paris race. However, Edward Wingfield died in 1764, before the Grand Hôtel de Monville was constructed. Therefore, Monville's guest would have been Richard Wingfield, 3rd Viscount Powerscourt (1730-1788).

[51] France was the first country to establish control over the islands. In French, the islands are known as Les Malouines, after the 250 colonists from the town of Saint-Malo, who established the settlement of Port Saint Louis in 1764.

[52] The two countries were at a diplomatic standoff and close to war. Choiseul wanted France to ally herself with Spain, but Louis XV refused, and the two belligerents reached an inconclusive compromise. The dispute was a precursor to the 1982 war between Britain and Argentina over the islands.

of war, was forced to retire to his estate, Chanteloup, near Amboise in the Loire Valley. The centerpiece of the property was a six-story Chinese-style pagoda, 44 meters (108 feet) high, built between 1775 and 1778. All the buildings were demolished in the 19th century save the pagoda, which survives to this day.

In April 1777, Monville hosted Joseph II, the Holy Roman Emperor and brother of Marie Antoinette, who was traveling in France incognito using the alias "Count Falkenstein." While in France, he was well received, and much flattered by the intellectuals he met, but his observations led him to predict, accurately, the approaching downfall of the French monarchy.

The English lexicographer and literary critic Dr. Samuel Johnson (1709-1784), who published the first dictionary of the English language in 1755, visited Monville's townhouse on October 11, 1775, escorted by the French architect and archaeologist Julien-David Le Roy (1724-1803), author of *Les Ruines des plus beaux monuments de la Grèce.* Le Roy was a friend of Monsieur de Monville and his book may have influenced Monville's designs for his country estate, the Désert de Retz.

The great conversationalist waxed less enthusiastic over the Grand Hôtel de Monville than Dufort de Cheverny, dismissing it as "furnished with effeminate and minute elegance." Dr. Johnson was accompanied on his trip by Henry and Hester Lynch

Thrale, who also visited the Grand Hôtel de Monville. The prudish Mrs. Thrale was even harsher than Dr. Johnson in her judgment, declaring in her journal on October 21, 1775, that the decors in Monville's residence were "contrived merely for the purposes of disgusting lewdness."

Two views of the Grand Hôtel de Monville, painted by Antoine-François Sergent and engraved by Joseph-Alexandre Le Campion, have been preserved in the Cabinet des Estampes of the Bibliothèque Nationale de France [53] along with a hundred of Boullée's futuristic drawings, bequeathed to the library at his death.

Sergent led a tumultuous life during the French Revolution, becoming involved in the political turmoil of the time and implicated in the massacres of September 1792 and the insurrection of May 1795 that resulted in his exile in Switzerland. He returned to France, along with many other exiles, in 1797, and died in 1847 at the age of 96.

Unfortunately, nothing remains of the Grand and Petit Hôtels de Monville; both were demolished in 1855 under the orders of civic planner Baron Georges Eugène Haussmann (1808-1891) in order to permit the construction of the Boulevard Malesherbes.

---

[53] The contemporary French aquarellist Christian Bénilan has depicted the Grand Hôtel de Monville c. 1774 as part of a series of historical buildings in and around Paris as they might have appeared before their destruction, published as *Paris autrefois*, in 2006.

For those wishing to gain an idea of what the Grand Hôtel de Monville may have looked like, Allan Braham, writing in *The Architecture of the French Enlightenment*, notes that the Hôtel Alexandre (or Hôtel Soult), dating from 1763, located at 16, Rue de la Ville l'Evêque in the Eighth Arrondissement of Paris, is the sole surviving building of a group of Boullée's private houses that included the Grand and Petit Hôtels de Monville.

Monville was an accomplished musician on the harp and the flute—and presumably other instruments as well—and a friend of many musicians. He was also a composer. The *Mercure de France*, in its issue of May 1757, reproduces the program of a concert of devotional music performed on May 10th, Easter Sunday: "...All the pieces were appropriate for the occasion. The concert began with the *First Sonata* by Monsieur Mondonville, followed by *Diligam te*, a motet for a large chorus by Monsieur Gilles...Madame Vistris-de Giardini sang two Italian arias and Mademoiselle le Miere and Monsieur Besche sang the first concerto for voice of Monsieur [de] Monville. Mr. Balbastre played one of his organ concertos."

In 1770, Monsieur de Monville published three of his musical works known as *ariettes*: "Les amours de village ou Lisette et Colin," "Habitants de ces bois" and "Le Rossignol par son ramage." In 1771, Monville published a collection of short chamber cantatas known as *cantatilles*: "Le Bonheur," "Le

Moment," "Le départ de Cloé" and "Le retour de Cloé." A third collection of Monville's *ariettes* and *cantatilles* would be published in 1775. [54]

On September 25, 2011, "Le retour de Cloé" was performed at the Désert de Retz by guitarist Didier Magne, accompanied by Huguette Géliot, harpist; Patricia Samuel, soprano and Serge Louet, flautist.

In addition to his skills as a musician and architect, Monsieur de Monville became renowned as an archer, using a polished, tempered steel bow with a black velvet grip. The Scots landscape architect Thomas Blaikie (1751-1838), who met Monville in the company of Louis Philippe Joseph, Duc d'Orléans, admitted that Monville was "the best archer in France and perhaps in Europe," but expressed his contempt for Monville, churlishly disdaining him as a "Pretended Connisseur [*sic*] in everything."

The *Mémoires Secrets pour Servir à l'Histoire de la République des Lettres* [55] report in an entry dated October 30, 1771, that Monville defended his

---

[54] A 155-page manuscript of *Ariettes pour la Harpe,* including Monville's works, once owned by Marie Elisabeth Chamillart, Marquise de Suze (1713-1788) may be consulted on Gallica. A facsimile edition was published in 2014.

[55] Published in 18 volumes between1783 and 1789, the *Mémoires Secrets* document political and cultural events between 1782 and 1787. Authorship is attributed to Louis Petit de Bachaumont (1690–1771), but it is unlikely that he was the actual author, since all volumes describe events which occurred after his death. The work is currently attributed to Mathieu-François Pidansat de Mairobert and Barthélemy-François-Joseph Mouffle d'Angerville and can be consulted on Gallica.

reputation by winning a contest held in the Bois de Boulogne. The Duc d'Orléans, one of Monville's hunting companions, wagered that Monville would be unable to kill a pheasant on the wing in ten attempts with his bow and arrow. In front of a great throng of spectators, Monville transfixed the first pheasant...but missed the nine others.[56]

---

[56] *Mémoires Secrets*, Tome Sixième, Pages 22-23.

The Désert de Retz

"The House of the Desert, belonging to M[r]. de Monville," by Constant Bourgeois (1767-1841), engraved by Felipe Cardano and reproduced in *Le Nouveau Jardin Français* by Alexandre de Laborde, published in 1808.

Recollect too… the Dessert[sic].
How grand the idea excited by the remains of such a column!
The spiral staircase too was beautiful.
--Thomas Jefferson, October 12, 1786

Louis XVI (1754-1793) was crowned on June 11, 1775, ruled as King of France and Navarre until 1791, and then as King of the French from 1791 to 1792, when he was deposed. He was executed in January 1793, and his queen, Marie Antoinette of Austria (1755-1793), the following October.

Succeeding Louis XV, his unpopular grandfather, Louis XVI was well aware of the growing opposition of the French population to the absolute monarchy. The first part of his reign was marked by his attempts to reform the kingdom in accordance with Enlightenment ideals. Serfdom and torture were eliminated and civil rights were granted to Protestants in 1787 and Jews in 1791.

Louis XVI supported the American insurgents who were seeking their independence from Great Britain, aiding them with money (France spent an estimated 1.3 billion *livres* to support the Americans directly), munitions and equipment and allowing many thousands of French volunteers to serve alongside the Americans in their fight for independence. To express their gratitude, in 1780, the Virginia General Assembly approved the charter of Louisville, naming the town in honor of Louis XVI,[57] and in 1788, a town named Marietta, in honor of Queen Marie Antoinette, was established at the confluence of the Muskingum and Ohio rivers.

---

[57] After the American Revolution, residents of Kentucky County, Virginia, petitioned for a separation from Virginia. Louisville, Virginia, therefore became Louisville, Kentucky, on June 1, 1792, when the Commonwealth of Kentucky was admitted to the Union as the fifteenth state.

In addition to Enlightenment ideals transforming politics and governance, a transformation was gradually taking place in the French landscape garden. The movement towards these new gardens was a reaction against the symmetrical, classical gardens such as those at Versailles and began in the late 16th and early 17th century, reaching a peak in the last half of the 18th century.

The first influence came from England where, in the first half of the 18th century, new gardens were laid out and descriptions of English landscape gardens and treatises by English authors were translated into French. Rousham, Oxfordshire, featured a false ruin known as the Eyecatcher; and Stourhead, Wiltshire, boasted a Pantheon, a temple dedicated to Apollo, and a 14th century market cross moved from Bristol.

Pavilions, statuary, a Corinthian Arch and a Temple of British Worthies decorated the Stowe Landscape Gardens in Buckinghamshire. This temple, an exedra created by the prominent architect William Kent (c.1685-1748), is decorated with busts of sixteen poets, philosophers, scientists, monarchs, statesmen and warriors, each accompanied by a text.

To entice and instruct French visitors, a guide entitled *Les Charmes de Stow* [*sic*], by "J. de C.," dedicated to an anonymous "Mademoiselle," was published in London in 1748. [58] Writing in an

---

[58] Only one copy of this work, whose origins are a mystery, is known to have survived. The full text, however, was reprinted in *Descriptions of Lord*

epistolary style with touching naiveté, the author conveys his wonderment at *"le lieu le plus enchanté de toute l'Angleterre."*

René-Louis de Girardin (1735-1808) visited Stowe in the mid-1760s. After his return to France, he settled in Ermenonville, where he constructed one of the first picturesque gardens in France; parts can be visited today. In 1761, Rousseau visited Stowe and other English gardens, and his writings helped spread their fame and influence throughout Europe. He wrote in *La Nouvelle Héloïse*:

> Stowe is composed of very beautiful and very picturesque spots chosen to represent different kinds of scenery, all of which seem natural except when considered as a whole, as in the Chinese gardens...The master and creator of this superb domain has also erected ruins, temples and ancient buildings, [which] like the scenes, exhibit a magnificence which is more than human.[59]

François-Joseph Bélanger (1744-1818), the architect who designed Bagatelle and Méréville, visited Stowe in 1777-1778 and drew the gardens. Also in 1777, the King's Geographer, Georges-Louis Le Rouge (1707-c.1790) published the second of his twenty-one volume *Détail des nouveaux jardins à la mode*, generally known as the *Cahiers des Jardins Anglo-Chinois*, that included engravings of the

---

Cobham's Garden at Stowe 1700-1750, edited by George B. Clarke, published by the Buckinghamshire Record Society in 1990.
[59] Cited in *Temples of Delight: Stowe Landscape Gardens*, by John Martin Robinson, The National Trust, 1990.

Temple of Venus, the Gothic Temple, the Temple to Modern Virtue and the Artificial Rockery at Stowe as well as structures in other important gardens in Britain, especially Kew.[60]

It is conceivable that Monsieur de Monville who, judging from the contents of his library, was conversant in English, may have been one of the French visitors to these gardens on a trip to England, either before or after the Seven Years' War, (1754-1763), in which France and England were belligerents, although no documentation confirming such a voyage is known to this author.

In the 1740's and 1750's, accounts of travels to China began appearing in English and French. The most influential of these was published in 1757 by Sir William Chambers (1723-1796), a Scotsman who traveled to China where he observed Chinese gardens architecture and decorative arts.

Chambers designed a landscape garden at Kew that included Chinese elements. In his discussion of gardens, he elaborated the Chinese idea that gardens should be composed of a series of scenes eliciting different emotions, ranging from enchantment to horror and laughter.

---

[60] In April 1786, Thomas Jefferson and John Adams traveled together, visiting a number of English gardens in what Abigail Adams described as their "journey into the country."

French painters, notably Hubert Robert, Claude Lorrain and Nicolas Poussin, with their renderings of Arcadian landscapes and mythological scenes, also exerted a powerful influence on the design of French gardens. Identified by the terms *jardins anglo-chinois,* *jardins pittoresques,* *jardins paysagers* and *jardins à l'anglaise,* they were intended to be allegories inspired by literature and painting, replete with symbols and hidden messages.

The gardens themselves were the ancestors of today's theme parks. They could be recreations of the Garden of Eden or evocations of the Arcadia of classical Roman mythology, chronologies of the history of mankind or microcosms of the principal nations and cultures of the world, such as the Désert de Retz.[61]   By the advent of the French Revolution, over a score of these gardens dotted the countryside surrounding Paris in the region known as Ile de France.

In 1774, Monville, now over forty years old, began acquiring property in the parish of Saint-Jacques-de-Retz,[62] a hamlet of several farms with a population

---

[61] A modern equivalent of an 18th century microcosm might be the World Showcase at the Epcot theme park in Florida, where eleven countries are represented by symbolic pavilions.

[62] The original orthography, dating from 1221, was Saint-Jacques-de-Roye. "Roye" evolved to "Rais" in the 17th century and finally became "Retz." Therefore, "Retz" should properly be pronounced *reh.* The Forêt de Retz is located in Picardy, northeast of Paris.   The Pays de Retz is a region of Brittany located in the *département* of Loire-Atlantique. Retz is also the name of a wine-growing town in Austria.

of around a hundred, located adjacent to the Forêt de Marly, where he would construct his celebrated picturesque garden, to be known, first, as Monsieur de Monville's Desert and, later, as the Désert de Retz. Monville would continue buying lots in 1776, 1777, 1779 and 1786; the total area of the estate would cover 38 hectares (roughly 100 acres). [63]

An entry in the *Mémoires Secrets* dated August 5, 1781, offers a brief description of Monville (misspelled "Mouville") as well as his Désert.

According to the memorialist:

> Monville is a wealthy individual in the capital, who, blessed with all the gifts that nature could bestow to which are joined all the talents that art could give him, and provided with the various things that can make an apparently happy man, is nevertheless, the most jaded mortal in France. At any rate, he supports this burden and shirks it as best as he is able.

The writer reports that "the most curious part of this thebaïd is its Château à la Chinoise," which, because of its new design, was declared accurate by visitors who had traveled China themselves. Two structures were under construction in 1781, a *"maison en fût de colonne"* and *"une porte en rocher."* The article concludes, "The Queen has gone there several times and greatly enjoys being there."

---

[63] Saint-Jacques-de-Retz was subsequently incorporated into the town of Chambourcy.

By 1786, a score of structures—some with historical, philosophical or symbolic meaning and others for practical purposes—would populate the estate. As Jean-Louis Saury observed, [64] "The Désert de Retz was a blending of the knowledge and curiosity of the 18th century French enhanced by the accounts of travelers to distant lands."

The most commonly-used term in French for these structures is *fabrique*, which is generally rendered in English as "folly," although the terms are not really analogous.

Charles Boot wrote in a review of a collection of essays entitled, *Experiencing the Garden in the Eighteenth Century*:

> ...[T]he visitor to an eighteenth-century garden was not only a spectator, but also an actor, himself or herself part of the changing compositions. Eighteenth-century gardens were intended by their creators as places where *meaning* was carefully encoded, often by indirect references or allusions. The various scenes or episodes within gardens, notably where there were what the French call *fabriques*, were intended to trigger responses in those who experienced them.[65]

The Désert de Retz is typical of the French landscape garden in that its structures symbolized extinct classical civilizations, exotic lands and rustic

---

[64] Saury, Jean-Louis, *Le Désert de Retz-Jardin des Lumières*, Chambourcy, 2009.

[65] The review can be accessed on the website of the Garden History Society.

73

virtues. What is exceptional about the Désert de Retz is that—despite the vicissitudes of time and the neglect of man—it remains, along with the Queen's Hamlet at Trianon, in the grounds of Versailles, the best-preserved example in France of an 18th century landscape garden.

The first structure of the Désert de Retz, the Temple of Pan, with a Doric peristyle, was completed in 1775. It was probably inspired by the 1st century BC Temple of Vesta at Tivoli, Italy, also the inspiration for the Temple of Modern Philosophy at Ermenonville, the creation of the painter Hubert Robert (1733-1808), and the Temple of Love at Trianon, designed by the landscape architect Richard Mique (1728-1794).[66]

Pan is the god of nature, hunting and rustic music, and was therefore an appropriate choice for a building surrounded by the wilderness of the Forêt de Marly, reserved as a royal hunting ground. The building remained in fairly good condition until the middle of the 20th century when the walls began to collapse. Partial consolidation was undertaken in the 1970's and a complete restoration was undertaken in 2012-2013.

After the Temple of Pan, construction continued on more structures, which would eventually include the

---

[66] Mique and his son were arrested for conspiring to save the life of Marie Antoinette; after a summary trial, both were executed on July 8, 1794 (20 Messidor II).

Chinese House, the Column House,[67] the Pyramid Icehouse, the Temple of Repose and an Open-air Theater as well as farm buildings, greenhouses, the Orangery, a physic garden and a kitchen garden.

Monsieur de Monville's Desert was destined to become his *résidence secondaire*, a refuge from the often insalubrious and malodorous environment of 18th century Paris, particularly during the summer months. After all, hadn't none other than Rousseau described Paris as a city of "noise, smoke and mud" in Book IV of *Emile?*

Monville did not only possess property in Paris and Chambourcy, however. According to Leroux-Cesbron, on December 23, 1774, Jean André Isnard, *bourgeois de Paris* and a former official in the court of Louis XV, sold Monsieur de Monville his "Petit Château," located on the left bank of the Seine on the Rue de la Saussage in Neuilly-sur-Seine, at that time a village and river port west of Paris.

A map published in 1772, conserved in the Neuilly Archives, shows the layout of the streets and the location of buildings, fields and vacant lots in the village, as well as the newly-inaugurated Pont de Neuilly, designed by Jean-Rodolphe Perronet (1708-

---

[67] Monsieur de Monville and his contemporaries referred to the building as *La Colonne détruite* (the Destroyed Column) or simply *La Colonne.* In France today, it is generally referred to as *La Colonne brisée*, in which *brisée* can be translated as "shattered," "ruined" or "broken." *Pace* Monville, the term "Column House" has been used throughout this text.

1794), the leading civil engineer in France. [68]

Additionally, two plates, numbers 4 and 5, in Cahier X of Georges-Louis Le Rouge's *Détail des nouveaux jardins à la mode*, depict *"la maison à M. de Monville"* beside the larger château. Several gardens, including a *potager* or kitchen garden, were laid out adjacent to the building; in front a series of terraces led down to the Seine. The property occupied a surface area of $4^{1}/_{2}$ *arpents*, corresponding to 1.53 hectares or 3.8 acres. Before it was acquired by Monsieur Isnard, the Petit Château was intended to be the principal residence of the eldest son of the Duc d'Orleans, the Duc de Chartres. [69]

On the south side of Monville's Petit Château was the domain originally owned by Anne-Nicolas-Robert de Caze (1718-1793), a retired tax farmer, who had transferred it to the noted antiquary and naturalist Aubin-Louis Millin de Grandmaison (1759-1818). On the north side of the property was the grandiose Château de Neuilly, with its grounds and outbuildings. In 1741, Marc-Pierre de Voyer de Paulmy d'Argenson (1696-1764), Minister of War under Louis XV, acquired the estate. The Count d'Argenson rebuilt the chateau in 1751 on the plans

---

[68] The agronomist Antoine Parmentier (1737-1813) advocated adding the potato to the human diet and set up an experimental potato patch in Neuilly in 1786 on a large tract of land donated by Louis XVI. Armed guards were posted around the plot during the day but removed at night: hungry Parisians stole the precious tubers, which rapidly became a staple.

[69] Leroux-Cesbron, Charles, *Le Château de Neuilly: Chronique d'un Château Royal*, Paris, Perrin, 1923.

of the architect Jean-Sylvain Cartaud (1675-1758). An annotation on plate 4 of Le Rouge's Cahier X specifies that the Petit Château was *"cy-devant à M. Isnard, Intendant du Roi,"* confirming its ownership by Monsieur Isnard who, at the time, was employed as Argenson's steward.

The Château de Neuilly and its grounds were purchased in 1766 following the death of the Count d'Argenson and modified by Claude-Pierre-Maximilien Radix de Sainte-Foix (1736-1810), a financier and politician. In 1768, Madame du Barry, then still known as Mademoiselle Lange, was the mistress of Radix when she was spotted by Louis XV; it was *"le coup de foudre,"* love at first sight, and Radix was promptly divested of the young beauty.

Radix had also acquired a reputation as a swindler: accused as early as 1780 by Louis XVI's Finance Minister Jacques Necker of embezzling five million *livres*, he absconded to London with his mistress, Mary Frances Henrietta Lachs de Saint-Albin, where they remained until the fall of the Bastille in 1789. Upon returning to Paris, he speculated in real estate, acquiring cheaply large estates in the provinces that had been confiscated by the government and were being sold off to raise funds.

In 1792, the same year that Monville sold his properties, Radix sold the Château de Neuilly, then invested the proceeds in England and lived comfortably off the income. [70] The purchaser was the *salonnière* and dramatist Madame de Montesson. Arrested and imprisoned on April 20, 1793 (1 Floréal II), she was released on September, 28, 1794 (7 Vendémiaire III), after the fall of Robespierre.

As for Radix, he was arrested and at first detained in the Conciergerie but, "for reasons of health," he was transferred to the Pension Belhomme, a *maison de santé*—a private clinic—on the Rue de Charonne converted into a detention center for wealthy prisoners, owned and operated by a joiner and mirror-maker named Jacques Belhomme. Radix remained in relative confort, fed, housed and cared for during seven months until his release on November 23, 1794 (3 Fimaire III). In fact, no inmate in Belhomme's custody was ever brought to trial.

Jacques Belhomme himself was arrested in January 1794 and received a sentence of six years for abusing his authority, overcharging his inmates and supplying them with wine. Pleading illness, he handed over the management of the business to his wife and was transferred to the Maison Coignard, another *maison de santé,* on the Rue de Picpus. Eugène Coignard's most notorious inmate was Donatien-Alphonse-François de Sade, who praised the facility in a letter to his agent, Gaspard-François-

---

[70] Not only were Radix and Monville neighbors, they had many friends in common, including Louis XVI's cousin, the Duc d'Orléans, and Bertrand Barère de Vieuzac. Both also banked with Jean-Frédéric Perregaux.

Xavier Gaufridi, as "*un paradis terrestre; belle maison, superbe jardin, societe choisie, d'aimables femmes.*" After the guillotine was relocated from what is now the Place de la Concorde to the Place du Trône Renversé—now the Place de la Nation—on June 14, 1794, the Maison Coignard's garden was converted into a mass grave for the decapitated bodies of its victims; it is now known as the Picpus Cemetery. Like Radix, both Belhomme and the Marquis de Sade cheated fate; their lives were spared by Robespierre's overthrow. Sade was released from custody in October 1794 and died in 1814. After Belhomme's sentence ended in 1798, he returned to manage his clinic. He died in 1827 and the building was razed in 1973.

According to Leroux-Cesbron, it was no more than a "passing fancy" for Monville to have bought his house in Neuilly-sur-Seine: "The caprice was of short duration, since Monville sold it two years later." In addition to the chapter on Monsieur de Monville, Leroux-Cesbron includes essays on Radix de Sainte-Foix and the Count d'Argenson and in his collection *Gens et Choses d'Autrefois*, published in 1914.

On July 26, 1776, François-Gaspard Maynaud [or Maynard] de Collonges, the colonel of a regiment of Dragoons, acquired Monville's residence in Neuilly-sur-Seine, then sold it shortly thereafter to Albertine Elisabeth de Champcenetz (née de Nyvenheim de Nieukerque (1742-1805), known as "La Belle Hollandaise." One of a myriad of Louis XV's

79

mistresses, she became the third wife of Jean Louis Quentin de Richebourg de Champcenetz (1723-1813), Governor of the Tuileries Palace.

A counter-revolutionary, La Belle Hollandaise was arrested in the Petit Château on February 9, 1794 (21 Pluviôse II), but survived the Reign of Terror. Her stepson, however, the political satirist Louis René Quentin de Richebourg de Champcenetz, born in 1760, was executed on the guillotine in 1794.

The Petit Château once owned by Monville was sold in 1821 to Louis-Philippe I (1773-1850), the last King of the French, who promptly razed it and erected a new building, also known as the Petit Château de Neuilly, on the premises. This building was demolished early in the 20th century.

In December 1776, Benjamin Franklin (1706-1790) had been dispatched to France as commissioner for the United States. He took with him his two grandsons, 16-year-old William Temple Franklin—known as Temple[71]—whom Franklin had engaged as his secretary, and nine-year old Benjamin Franklin Bache—nicknamed Benny—the son of Franklin's daughter Sarah. The party arrived in the Breton port of Aurey on December 21, 1776. This was Benjamin Franklin's third trip to France, after

---

[71] Temple was born in London in 1760, the illegitimate son of Benjamin Franklin's illegitimate son, William Franklin, the last colonial governor of New Jersey. Temple's mother is unknown.

previous brief visits in 1767 and 1769.[72]

Franklin and his grandsons lived in what was then the village of Passy, described by the historian Claude-Anne Lopez in her book, *Mon Cher Papa: Franklin and the Ladies of Paris*, as "a conglomeration of villas and châteaux hidden among woods and vineyards." Their residence was the Hôtel de Valentinois, placed at their disposal and fully staffed by Jacques-Donatien Le Ray de Chaumont (1726–1803) who had purchased the property from Jacques-Philippe de Choiseul-Stainville, the husband of Monsieur de Monville's niece Thomasse-Thérèse, only a few months before Franklin's arrival. Chaumont was an aristocratic shipping magnate[73] and one of the most fervent of the many French "Fathers of the American Revolution." He later opposed the excesses of the French Revolution, but managed to survive the Reign of Terror. His son of the same name, known in America as James Le Ray, emigrated to the United States, where he married Grace Coxe of Sidney, NJ, on February 21, 1790, and subsequently founded the town of Le Ray, in Jefferson County, NY, where they settled.

Benjamin Franklin first enrolled Benny in Le Cœur's, a Parisian boarding school, where one of his

---

[72] Franklin crossed the Atlantic eight times, in an age when the average person never strayed more than twenty miles from his home during a lifetime.

[73] Whereas Monville had been Grand Master of Waters and Forests for Normandy, Le Ray de Chaumont held the same position for Berry.

classmates was John Quincy Adams (1767-1848), the son of John and Abigail Adams (1744-1818) and the future sixth president of the United States. After a few months, however, Franklin sent Benny to Geneva, "so that he might become a Republican and a Protestant which in the French schools would not have been possible." Back in Paris, Benny also studied type-founding as an apprentice to François-Ambrose Didot (1730-1804), a printer, publisher and typographer.

Franklin first served as a representative of the American colonies, along with Silas Dean and Arthur Lee, and entered into secret negotiations with the French government in order to secure financial aid and military supplies for the United States.

The main negotiator on the French side was Monville's close friend, Beaumarchais. However, because France was still officially at peace with England, and Louis XVI was unwilling to go to war, the French could not openly supply aid to the Americans.

Consequently, in June 1777, Beaumarchais set up a shell organization called Roderigue Hortalez & Compagnie. Louis XVI loaned the firm one million *livres* and convinced his cousin, Carlos III of Spain, to put up a similar amount. Hortalez would buy surplus military supplies from French arsenals and then resell them to the American insurgents with return payment of American products, primarily tobacco. The cover would effectively conceal Louis XVI's involvement in the operation.[74]

Dr. George R. Fisher wrote in his online history *Philadelphia Reflections,* [75] "By September 1777, Beaumarchais had shipped five million *livres* worth of supplies to America without repayment."

Beaumarchais requested compensation from the American Congress after the war, but his requests were denied. [76] Thirty-six years after his death, Beaumarchais's heirs were compensated with a portion of the original debt.

Fisher concluded, "In effect Beaumarchais nearly single-handedly supplied the American Revolution with arms receiving very little in return except his financial ruin."

In addition to Beaumarchais, who was supplying munitions to the American revolutionaries, many idealistic French officers—mostly from the nobility—crossed the Atlantic with their troops to volunteer in the Continental Army. Some joined

---

[74] The modern euphemism for such subterfuge—the withholding of information from senior officials in order to protect them from repercussions should illegal activities become public knowledge—is "plausible deniability."

[75] Fisher, George R., *Philadelphia Reflections*. http://www.philadelphia-reflections.com/

[76] Congress disputed the amount claimed. Additionally, the Treasury was virtually empty since, under the Articles of Confederation (1781-1789), Congress had no power to raise money through taxation.

even before the Battle of Bunker Hill in 1775.

At least eighty-seven officers of the French Royal Army served in the Continental Army, and several French army or naval officers served with John Paul Jones's naval squadron. In all, ten infantry regiments with between 12,000 and 15,000 French soldiers fought alongside their American comrades-in-arms in the Revolutionary War.[77]

Warrington Dawson (1878-1962), in a study sponsored by the Société des Américainistes, published in 1936 an Honor Roll listing the names, dates and places of birth and dates and places of death of 2,112 French soldiers who gave their lives fighting for American freedom between 1771 and 1783.

The most preëminent of the French officers was the Marquis de Lafayette who, at the age of twenty, defied the king's orders and enlisted to serve with the Americans. On April 20, 1777, he sailed for America, disguised as a woman. After serving with distinction as a major general, he returned to France

---

[77] The Chasseurs-Volontaires de Saint-Domingue was a volunteer regiment made up of ten companies of light infantry enlisted from "free men of color" recruited in the then-French colony of Saint-Domingue or Hispaniola, now Haiti and the Dominican Republic, under the command of Admiral Charles-Henri d'Estaing who fought against the British during the siege of Savannah, GA. With an estimated 545 men, it was the largest unit of men of African descent to fight in the American Revolution. The future king of Haiti, Henri Christophe, twelve years old at the time, served with the regiment as a drummer-boy. Charles-Henri d'Estaing was sent to the guillotine on April 28, 1794 (9 Floréal II). Henri Christophe committed suicide with a silver bullet to the heart on October 8, 1820.

in 1781 to great acclaim and entered politics. Fifty years later, upon the invitation of President James Monroe, he returned to America and embarked on a triumphal tour of all twenty-four states. Because of his service to both France and America, Lafayette was known as "the Hero of the Two Worlds." On August 6, 2002, an act of Congress proclaimed Lafayette an honorary citizen of the United States.[78]

The Comte de Rochambeau (1725-1807) was the commander-in-chief of the 5,500-man French Expeditionary Force—in fact, he had more troops under his command than Washington. Admiral François Joseph Paul de Grasse (1722-1788) commanded the French fleet at the Battle of the Chesapeake, preventing the British from resupplying their troops. This naval blockade, combined with the ground forces of Rochambeau, Lafayette and Washington, led directly to the Surrender of General Charles Cornwallis (1738-1805) at Yorktown, VA., on September, 22, 1781.[79]

Major Pierre-Charles L'Enfant (1754-1825) was recruited by Beaumarchais to serve as a military engineer with Lafayette. He would subsequently lay out the street plan of Washington, DC, basing it on the design of the château and gardens of Versailles.

---

[78] Lafayette was entombed in the Picpus Cemetery in Paris, where an American flag always flies over his grave. During the Nazi occupation of Paris during World War II, the flag was never removed.

[79] In the French Cemetery at Yorktown lie the remains of 50 unknown French soldiers killed during the hostilities.

After the war, in 1783, a number of officers who had served at least three years in the Continental Army or Navy, including 14 officers of the French Army and Navy, formed the Society of the Cincinnati to preserve the ideals of the Revolutionary War. George Washington served as the first President General of this veterans' organization, from December 1783 until his death in 1799.

The society derives its name from Cincinnatus, the Roman general, who saved Rome from destruction and then quietly retired to his farm. It honored the ideal of return to civilian life by military officers following the Revolution rather than imposing military rule on the nation. However, distrust and opposition arose because membership in the society was hereditary; some people, including Franklin, thought that the members of the Cincinnati would become an aristocracy and therefore a threat to democracy. For that reason, the organization almost disappeared for more than a century. Today, revived, its headquarters are located in Anderson House, on Massachusetts Avenue, NW—Embassy Row—in Washington, DC.[80]

One may wonder what Monville's connection with the American Revolution might have been. Certainly there is no evidence of any direct involvement; however, a number of the principal

---

[80] In 1790, Arthur St. Clair, the governor of the Northwest Territory, named a settlement on the north side of the Ohio River "Cincinnati" in honor of the Society of the Cincinnati, of which he was president.

individuals instrumental in achieving France's support for American independence were Monville's close friends and associates.

Franklin represented the United States in negotiating the Treaty of Paris ending the Revolutionary War and establishing the independence of the United States. Peace negotiations began in April of 1782, involving Franklin, John Jay,[81] Henry Laurens[82] and John Adams on the American side and David Hartley[83] and Richard Oswald representing George III. The treaty was signed on September 3, 1783, by Franklin, Adams, Jay and Hartley.

Also present at the signing were Laurens and Temple Franklin. In his painting representing the event, Benjamin West depicted the five members of the American delegation; the British emissaries declined to pose, and the work was never completed. It is currently on display in the Winterthur Museum in Wilmington, DE.

---

[81] Jay (1745-1829) was serving as United States minister to Spain. After his return to America, he served as the first Chief Justice of the United States, presiding over the Supreme Court.

[82] Laurens (1724-1792), from South Carolina, was a partner in the largest slave-trading house in America. On his way to represent the United States in the Netherlands in 1780, he was captured by the British and held in the Tower of London, the only American to have been imprisoned there. He was released on December 31, 1781, in exchange for General Charles Cornwallis. He was also the first American to be cremated.

[83] In 1776 Hartley (1732-1814) was the first Member of Parliament to oppose the slave trade as being "contrary to the laws of God and the rights of men."

During his stay in France, Benjamin Franklin was active as a Freemason. Both Franklin and John Paul Jones were brethren of a lodge called Les Neuf Sœurs[84] that was influential in organizing French support for the American Revolution. On April 4, 1778—a month before his death—Voltaire was accompanied by his friend Franklin and inducted into the lodge in the presence of 250 prominent Masons; the philosopher was accepted as an Entered Apprentice Freemason. Franklin became Worshipful Master of the Lodge in 1779, and was reëlected in 1780, serving until his return to the United States in1781.

John Paul Jones[85] (1747-1792) was another of those exceptional American expatriates who were contemporaries of Monsieur de Monville and may have met him. Born in Scotland, Jones led a turbulent life as a sailor, first on British ships and then, after emigrating to America in the early 1770's, with the Continental Navy. Sailing for France in 1777, Jones met with Benjamin Franklin, John Adams and Arthur Lee, and developed a close friendship with Franklin that resulted in his induction into Les Neuf Sœurs in 1778. After a number of misadventures at the helm of the *USS Ranger*, Jones took command in 1779 of the 42-gun

---

[84] "Les Neuf Sœurs" refers to the nine muses: Calliope, Clio, Erato, Euterpe, Melpomene, Polyhymnia, Terpsichore, Thalia and Urania.

[85] He was born John Paul, but added "Jones" later.

Bonhomme Richard[86] a merchant ship rebuilt and donated to America by Jacques-Donatien Le Ray de Chaumont, the shipowner who had offered lodging to Benjamin Franklin and his grandsons. On September 23, 1779, Jones engaged the 50-gun British frigate, *HMS Serapis,* off the coast of England. As every American schoolboy knows, in the heat of battle, when the British admiral demanded that Jones surrender, he retorted, "I have not yet begun to fight."

After his great victory, John Paul Jones returned to a hero's welcome in Paris; he was especially lionized by the ladies, among them Queen Marie Antoinette, who received him at court.[87] Jones told his friend Benjamin Franklin that he wanted to learn French, so Franklin recommended that he learn with a "sleeping dictionary," that turned out to be Madame de Chaumont, the wife of Franklin's benefactor!

The following year, Louis XVI bestowed a knighthood on Jones—thenceforth Jones added "Chevalier" to his name—and awarded him a gold sword. After briefly returning to America, Jones retired in France where he died on July 18, 1792, at the age of 45, lonely and penniless, in his apartment at 19, rue de Tournon, in the Sixth Arrondissement of Paris. Gouverneur Morris, who had succeeded William Short as the minister plenipotentiary of the

---

[86] Jones named the ship in honor of Franklin's *Poor Richard's Almanac.*

[87] British chapbooks, an early form of dime novels, pictured Jones as a ruthless, marauding pirate.

United States to France, disliked Jones, as he as well as another American patriot, Thomas Paine, and refused to pay for—or even attend—Jones's funeral. Instead, the French National Assembly granted Jones a state funeral with full honors.

It has been written elsewhere that Benjamin Franklin visited the Désert de Retz in 1776. This assertion is erroneous. As noted previously, Franklin was appointed Commissioner for the United States in France in early December 1776 and did not arrive in France until December 21, 1776. Furthermore, this author has been unable to find substantiation for any visit during Franklin's nine-year tenure in Paris, either in his *Autobiography,* Walter Isaacson's authoritative *Benjamin Franklin: An American Life*, published in 2003, or among the 171,000 documents, including the personal papers of Franklin, posted by the National Archives on its Founders Online website.

It is conceivable, however, that Franklin met Monville at one of the many salons they both attended, such as that of Madame Helvétius, and that Franklin may have subsequently been invited to either the Grand Hôtel de Monville or the Désert de Retz.

Additionally, Claude-Anne Lopez notes that Madame Helvétius was always solicitous towards the septuagenarian Franklin, who was afflicted with frequent bouts of painful and incapacitating gout. She "organized little trips to the surroundings of

Paris: Marly, Chaillot, Choisy, St.-Germain, always including some young company for Temple." Given the multiplicity of Franklin's and Monville's shared interests, it is entirely possible if not likely that one of these excursions included a visit to the Désert de Retz.

Among the interests Monville and Franklin shared was a love of music. Monville was an accomplished harpist, flautist and composer, whereas Franklin, as an amateur, enjoyed playing the harp, the guitar and the violin and, in 1761, invented a musical instrument, a type of crystallophone called the armonica that would certainly have intrigued Monsieur de Monville.

The armonica consisted of a series of glasses blown in the shape of hemispheres, ranging in diameter from three to nine inches, with an iron spindle passing through holes in the middle of all the glasses. The player, sitting before the instrument, revolved the spindle with a treadle and touched the edges of the moving glasses to produce notes and chords. The armonica became popular in Europe; Marie Antoinette, still in Vienna, learned to play it, and both Mozart and Beethoven composed for it.[88]

There is some speculation that Monville was also a Freemason and that the structures at the Désert de Retz possess Masonic symbolism similar to that of

---

[88] Franklin's descendants donated an original armonica to the Franklin Institute in Philadelphia in 1956 and, in 1975, the Bakken Museum in Minneapolis acquired an armonica from the Brillon de Jouy family.

the Parc Monceau in Paris, designed by Carmontelle and built as an initiatory space by the Duc d'Orléans, a prominent Freemason in pre-Revolutionary France, and one of Monville's closest friends.

Despite the fact that Monville had many Masonic acquaintances, it is significant that his name does not appear on the membership rolls of any of the Masonic lodges operating in late 18th century Paris. There can be no doubt, however, that Monville shared some of the Freemasons' philosophy.

During the 17th and 18th centuries the tree of Freemasonry flourished and the trunk sprouted many different branches on both sides of the Channel. Anthony Vidler writes in his essay, "The Architecture of the Lodges: Rituals and Symbols of Freemasonry," that "By 1778 there were at least eighty-two lodges active in Paris alone…the Grand Orient counted some 8,500 members in the capital [out of an estimated population of 600,000], and beyond these were the schismatics of the Grand Lodge, a large number of military lodges for officers, women's lodges…together with hundreds of breakaway and autonomous sects." Vidler later notes that, because of the symbolic association of architecture with Freemasonry, "Between 1774 and 1789, over 120 architects belonged to lodges in Paris affiliated with the Grand Orient" and "The Neuf Sœurs Lodge… [included] five architects in its membership."

One branch of the Masonic movement was known

as Free Gardeners *(Les Francs-Jardiniers)*. Founded in Scotland in the mid-17ᵗʰ century, the movement spread to England and Ireland. Since Monville was passionately interested in gardening, botany and horticulture, it would be natural to conclude that he might have been a Free Gardener. But the movement never spread to France.

A Masonic movement that, unlike the Free Gardeners, was widespread in 18ᵗʰ century France was Woodmen Freemasonry *(La Franc-maçonnerie du Bois* or *la Franc-maçonnerie Forestière)*. The movement was founded in 1747 by Charles François Radet de Beauchesne and gained popularity among the landed aristocracy of the Ancien Régime. Rather than occult or philosophical speculations or political debates, members in these lodges indulged in gastronomic and secular pleasures. Since Monsieur de Monville had served as Grand Master of Waters and Forests for Normandy in 1756 and held the post until 1763, it is only natural to imagine that he might have been attracted to the Woodmen,[89] although his biography suggests that Monville was interested in more than just social gatherings.

Yet another philosophical club that attracted many members during the late 18ᵗʰ century in France was the *Cercle Social*, also known as *Les Amis de la Vérité*, described by the late French historian Albert

---

[89] A similar fraternal society, the Woodmen of the World, was founded in 1890 in Omaha, NE, by Joseph Cullen Root. It became known for its unique tombstones, in the shape of a tree stump. Today it owns and operates a large insurance company for its 800,000 members.

Soboul as "a combination of a revolutionary political club, a Masonic lodge and a literary salon." This movement attracted approximately 3,000 followers, of whom an estimated 130 were prominent personalities in the political scene before and during the French Revolution, including Condorcet, Lafayette, Jacques-Pierre Brissot (1754-1793) and Jérôme Pétion de Villeneuve (1756-1794), who defeated Lafayette in an election and became the second mayor of Paris, serving from 1791 to 1792. This organization published a newsletter known as *La Bouche de Fer*, whose pages were filled with political commentary written by its founders.

One of the best-known members of the *Cercle Social*, the orator and parliamentarian Bertrand Barère de Vieuzac (1755-1841), was most certainly known to Monville, because he was a frequent guest at the literary and musical salon hosted by Madame de Genlis, to whom Monville had once proposed marriage and with whom he remained in contact throughout his life.

Barère[90] was another of the colorful but essentially forgotten personages of revolutionary France. Because of his acquaintance with Madame de Genlis, he accompanied her to London along with three of her wards, among them Adélaïde d'Orléans (1777-1847), one of the twin daughters of the Duc

---

[90] He dropped "de Vieuzac" after titles of nobility were abolished in France on June 19, 1790.

d'Orléans, in October-November 1791. In addition to the *Cercle Social*, Barère belonged to another political club led by Brissot, the *Société des amis des Noirs* (1788-1793) that opposed slavery and the slave trade.[91]

On September 29, 1792, Barère was elected as one of the members of a committee, including Condorcet, Brissot, Thomas Paine and Pétion,[92] charged with drafting a new Constitution.

Bertrand Barère can be considered a key member of Monsieur de Monville's circle of acquaintances, since the two had so many friends in common. It is therefore reasonable to conclude that some of Barère's views, such as his opposition to slavery, were shared by Monville, and that Barère discussed with Monville the ideas incorporated into the Constitution,[93] including those of Paine.

Barère was the quintessential political survivor who always knew which way the winds were blowing. A one-time supporter of Robespierre, he was

---

[91] On February 4, 1794 (16 Pluviôse II), the French National Assembly emancipated all colonial slaves. Slavery was reinstituted under Napoleon Bonaparte in 1802 and not finally abolished in France until 1848.

[92] Pétion committed the fatal error of opposing Robespierre and fled Paris in June 1794, seeking refuge in the wine-producing town of Saint-Emilion. Advised that his arrest was imminent, he preferred suicide to the guillotine; his corpse was found in a field, "half-devoured by wolves."

[93] The *Constitution of the Year I* was adopted by referendum under universal male suffrage, winning 1,784,377 out of approximately 1,800,000 voters, and promulgated on June 24, 1793. Suspended during the Reign of Terror, it never entered into force.

amnestied by Napoleon Bonaparte and lived to the age of eighty-five; his memoirs were published posthumously in 1843.

Although the case can be made that Monville might have been an "Ami de la Vérité," it still appears unlikely, given the fact that Monville scrupulously avoided any public political activity or any involvement in the political ferment and turmoil surrounding him. In this respect, he was what his contemporaries would have described as *sage*. In fact, Monville's knowledge of the vicissitudes of Barère's political fortunes may have been a contributing factor to his abstinence from political clubs and movements.

The most likely Masonic movement that might have attracted Monville was a secretive brotherhood whose members were known as *Chevaliers du Noble Jeu de l'Arc* (The Knights of Noble Archery), whose unifying theme was perpetuating the ancient practice. This brotherhood, which appeared in France during the 17th century, recruited its members by invitation only, and postulants underwent initiatory rituals before being inducted. Other practices included esoteric teachings founded on symbols relative to archery as well as a number of rites and traditions derived from nautical and Masonic sources.

Monsieur de Monville would have been an ideal candidate for membership in the brotherhood of the Knights of Noble Archery. His prowess in archery is an undisputed fact, as has been noted previously, specifically his successful wager against the Duc d'Orléans.

What we might surmise about the demonstration in the Bois de Boulogne is that, since Monville won the bet—transfixing the pheasant on the first attempt—he simply missed the subsequent nine shots on purpose. If so, this suggests that Monville was indeed following the principles of the brotherhood, which required its members to "hold their tongue, respect the rules of courtesy, propriety and decorum and come to the aid of their brothers in misfortune."[94]

What also suggests that Monville may have been a member of the Knights of Noble Archery is that its membership lists were never written down. Thus, we know that Monville was an accomplished archer—perhaps the best in Europe—and that he was attracted to Masonic philosophy. Thus the fact that his name does *not* appear on the registers of any Masonic lodges may just be evidence confirming that he *was* a Chevalier du Noble Jeu de l'Arc. That is a paradox that most probably would have pleased Monsieur de Monville.

Diana Ketcham considers Anthony Vidler's essay, "the fullest and most balanced account of the Masonic gardens," and notes that Vidler "maintains

---

[94] For an extensive discussion of this lodge, see Pierre-Yves Beaurepaire, *Nobles jeux de l'Arc et loges maçonniques dans la France des Lumières-Enquête sur une sociabilité en mutation*, Éditions Ivoire-Clair, 2002.

a distinction between those that can be read as Masonic allegories and those that functioned as settings for Masonic ritual." It is evident that the Désert de Retz was allegorical rather than ritualistic. Monsieur de Monville appears to have been more of an esoterist than a Freemason.

Like many Frenchmen of his day, Monville was an admirer of and fascinated by the United States, the nascent republic on the other side of the Atlantic. Terra-cotta, slate-colored medallions of Benjamin Franklin and George Washington were discovered in the Column House and duly noted in the detailed inventory conducted by François Corborand and several other citizens after the Désert de Retz was confiscated in 1793.

Benjamin Franklin remained in France until 1785, when he returned to America and was succeeded as American ambassador in France by Thomas Jefferson. Franklin was elected as the sixth President of Pennsylvania in 1787 and died on April 17, 1790, at the age of 84. He left such a profound legacy in France and was so beloved by the French people that on June 14, 1790, the French National Assembly declared three days of mourning in his honor. Franklin became a hero in France just as Lafayette had in America.

Benjamin Franklin bequeathed William Temple Franklin his papers and correspondence, and appointed him as his literary executor. Temple edited and published editions of his grandfather's writings, including his *Autobiography*. Curiously the work was first published in French, in 1791. When the first English version was published in London in 1793, "anecdotes" by Brissot, Condorcet and Le Roy were appended.

After speculating in real estate in America, Temple Franklin relocated to France. He died in 1823 and was inhumed in the Père Lachaise Cemetery in Paris. Because he spent so much time in France, it is also likely that Temple Franklin may have visited the Désert de Retz, with or without his grandfather.

Benjamin Franklin's other grandson, Benjamin Franklin Bache, eventually returned to Philadelphia, where he became a publisher, opposed the Alien and Sedition Acts as unconstitutional, was briefly jailed, and died from yellow fever at the age of 29 in 1798.

The period between 1777 and 1778 saw a frenzy of construction at the Désert de Retz. Monsieur de Monville commissioned the Temple of Repose, the Hermitage, the Chinese House, greenhouses, the Orangery and the Obelisk. Nothing remains of any of these structures today except the four rusticated columns from the Temple of Repose, which have been moved from their original location, now part of a golf course adjacent to the garden.

In its design, Monville's Temple of Repose resembles the temple at the gardens of Betz, [95] in Picardy, north of Paris, designed by Hubert Robert for Maria-Caterina Brignole, Princess of Monaco (1737-1813), and mother of Prince Joseph, who was married to Monville's ill-starred grandniece, Françoise-Thérèse.

The Temple of Repose at Betz consisted of a circular room behind a façade with a semicircular settee inside. Unlike the Princess's temple, however, Monville's consisted of no more than a façade positioned on the circumference of a circle of trees. Nothing remains today of Monville's Hermitage which, for whatever reason, Le Rouge failed to illustrate in his Cahier XIII, entirely devoted to the Désert de Retz, published in 1785. [96]

However, there was a rustic, neo-Romanesque hermitage in the park at Betz. [97] Monville's longtime friend, Bertrand Barère de Vieuzac, who fancied himself a moral philosopher, visited Betz on ten occasions in late August and early September 1788. His detailed descriptions of each of the structures in the garden are complemented by aesthetic and

---

[95] Pronounced, in English, *beh.*

[96] Cahier XIII has been reproduced *in extenso* in the books about the Désert de Retz by Cendres and Radiguet and Diana Ketcham. All 21 volumes may be consulted on Gallica.

[97] Two etchings by Jacques-Simon Chéreau (176?-1808) of the Hermitage and one of the Chinese House at Betz are in the collection of the Musée de l'Ile de France in Sceaux.

philosophical reflections from his contemplative walks, recorded in a dozen letters that were not published until 2006, after their discovery by a scholar researching her doctoral thesis.[98]

Barère not only describes the building itself, but accords us the favor of reporting his extended conversation with Brother Alexis, the anchorite whom Maria-Caterina had engaged to reside on the premises and obey a set of rules she had drafted. The hermit explained to his interlocutor that he subsisted on the fruits and vegetables he cultivated in his garden, mostly carrots, cabbage and potatoes. Asked if he feared death, Brother Alexis responded that although he had some apprehensions, he had even more hope, and because of that, he wasn't concerned about dying. After the interview, the hermit offered Barère a guided tour of his modest abode.

Another of Monville's *fabriques*, the Chinese House, survived much longer than he could ever have imagined, but suffered substantial damage and a sad fate through neglect. Photographs from the late 19th century and the first half of the 20th century depict the Chinese House in perfect condition.

An American author, Marie Goebel Kimball (1889-1955), recounted in 1950 an amusing if purely imaginary anecdote that after the end of World War II, American soldiers hastened the structure's

---

[98] Barère's text is reproduced in *Polia, Revue de l'Art des Jardins*, No. 6, Automne 2006.

demise when they "decided to use the funny old shack as a target for pistol practice."[99]

Two years later, the Désert de Retz was visited by John Harris, an English writer on architecture, who described some of the interior decorations of the Chinese House. The visit was unauthorized and Harris cowered with fright in a corner of the house when he heard the barking of the caretaker's dogs, but his presence was not discovered.[100]

For lack of maintenance and upkeep, however, the Chinese House began to collapse in the 1960's. When the author of this book first visited the Désert de Retz in 1973, nothing was left of the Chinese House save a few rotting teak beams and panels engraved with *faux* Chinese characters, strewn on the ground in disarray and covered with exotic mushrooms.[101]

Although Monville's Chinese House was not the first Chinese-inspired construction in Europe, it was the first Chinese-style dwelling. Monville would be

---

[99] Kimball, Marie Goebel, *Jefferson: The Scene of Europe 1784-1789*, Coward-McCann, 1950.

[100] Harris's visit is described in Chapter 11, "Privé-Défense d'Entrer" of *Echoing Voices: More Memories of a Country House Snooper*, London, John Murray, 2002. He visited the Désert de Retz again—officially—in 1986.

[101] The characters may be real. Plaques on the Chinese House at Stowe were also decorated with characters originally thought to be *faux*; it was later learned that they were reproductions of illustrations in Sir William Chambers's *Designs of Chinese Buildings*.

able to occupy this building during the summer months or whenever he left his Paris residence to spend time in his country estate. When the Column House was completed in 1781, it may have replaced the Chinese House as the principal residence of the Désert de Retz. Historian Allan Braham speculates that Monville preferred to live in the comfort of the Chinese House, reserving the Column House for his guests.

Monville invited many guests to his garden, among them aristocrats and actresses, painters and writers, musicians and financiers. The *Mémoires Secrets* indicate that, although located six leagues from Paris, the garden attracted flocks of visitors; members of the general public could visit the garden if they were bought a ticket at the entrance and were "upstanding individuals." Following the example of Louis XIV, who had written a *Manière de Montrer les jardins de Versailles*, visitors were invited to follow a programmed itinerary, and such is still the case today.

Monsieur de Monville liked to invite a few friends for readings in the library, located on the upper story of the Chinese House, redolent with the spicy aromas of mahogany emanating from the woodwork and tea from a Sèvres porcelain service. Particularly popular were recitations from the *Rêveries du Promeneur Solitaire* by Rousseau and articles from the *Encyclopédie*, edited by Denis Diderot and Jean Le Rond d'Alembert. Published from 1751 to 1772, the immense work comprised 16,500 pages, 72,000 articles, and over 17,000,000 words. The editors wanted to incorporate all of the world's knowledge into the *Encyclopédie* and, like Jimmy Wales, creator of the Wikipedia, they hoped that the text could disseminate all this information to the public and to future generations.

Another attraction in Monville's Chinese House was a mechanical jumping frog with a Chinese mounted on its back. The 18th century saw the development of automata, or self-operating machines. French, German, English and Swiss watchmakers fabricated androids and mechanical animals such as Monville's frog. The world's first successfully-functioning biomechanical automaton is considered to be *The Flute Player*, invented by the French engineer Jacques de Vaucanson (1709-1782) in 1737. He also constructed the *Digesting Duck*, made of gilded copper which quacked, ate and drank, digested its food and gave the illusion of defecating like a living duck. [102] Henri Maillardet (1745-1830), a Swiss mechanician, created an automaton capable of drawing four pictures and writing three poems. Its origin was unknown when it arrived in pieces at the Franklin Institute in Philadelphia in 1928. When restored in 2007, it penned the words "written by the

---

[102] The original duck was apparently lost in a fire in Kraków in the mid-19th century, but a replica was created by Frédéric Vidoni in 1998 for the Musée des Automates in Grenoble.

automaton of Maillardet." [103]

Perhaps the most illustrious of the creators of the automata was the brilliant mathematician Pierre Jaquet-Droz (1721-1790). His three doll automata, the *Musician*, the *Draftsman* and the *Writer*, built between 1768 and 1774, are among the most remarkable 18th century automata.

The *Writer* is the most complex of the three automata. He is able to write any custom text up to 40 letters long. The text is coded on a wheel where characters are selected one by one. The writer uses a goose feather to write, which he inks from time to time, including a shake of the wrist to prevent ink from spilling. His eyes follow the text being written, and his head moves when he inks his quill. [104]

Perhaps the automaton that would have most pleased Monsieur de Monville was one made by London clockmaker Timothy Williamson (active 1769-1788) in 1780 for the Emperor of China: a seated android, dressed in European clothing, uses a brush to write eight Chinese characters on a scroll. The text transliterated reads *wan shou wu jiang* and translates as "boundless longevity."

---

[103] It is the inspiration for the broken automaton in Martin Scorsese's film, *Hugo*.

[104] All three automata are on permanent display at the Musée d'Art et d'Histoire in Neuchâtel, Switzerland.

Monville's contemporaries known to have visited the Désert de Retz included the poet Jacques Delille, who published his *Jardins, ou l'art d'embellir les paysages* in 1782; the poet and playwright Marie-Joseph Blaise de Chenier (1764-1811), and Hubert Robert, who specialized not only in painting picturesque gardens such as Monville's, but in designing them. He collaborated in designing the park of the château of Méréville, built for the wealthy financier Jean-Joseph de Laborde (1724-1794). Méréville was, along with the Désert de Retz, one of the finest folly gardens in France in its heyday, requiring almost 700 workers ten years to complete. Very little of the Parc de Méréville exits today; several of the structures, including a cenotaph dedicated to Captain James Cook, were transferred to the grounds of the château of Jeurre, where they can be seen today.[105]

Another guest was Claude Joseph Dorat, a poet, novelist, and playwright who, it is said, never changed a line. He wrote some of his works while in residence at the Désert de Retz. Dorat's books were lavishly illustrated by well-known artists; he squandered a substantial amount of his inheritance producing and self-publishing his works.

In 1777, Monville ordered a total of 4,050 exotic plants from the Royal Nurseries to decorate his

---

[105] Laborde's son Alexandre (1773-1842) wrote and published at his expense numerous works, including a folio, *Le Nouveau Jardin Français,* the source of the illustrations in this book.

garden and planted exotic trees and shrubs imported from all over the world. Varieties included poplar, horse chestnut, ash, Judas tree, St. Lucia cherry, bladder senna, dogwood, sumac and elderberry.

Monsieur de Monville also preserved an ancient layered linden tree, still standing and now estimated to be 450 years old, located between the Column House and the Pyramid Icehouse. On October 3, 2010, at a ceremony was held at the Désert de Retz, a plaque was dedicated identifying the tree as an *"Arbre Remarquable de France."*

Since none of the farm buildings remain today, and since Monsieur de Monville's estate has been truncated to half its original size, visitors today tend to ignore the fact that the Désert de Retz was not only a picturesque garden with its evocation of disparate civilizations, but also a working farm complete with orchards, herds of livestock, a botanical garden, greenhouses and poultry coops. At the time of the property's sale in 1792, it was maintained by a staff of twenty-five employees, some of whom commuted from the adjoining communities of Saint-Nom-la-Bretèche and Saint-Germain-en-Laye.

Thanks to François Corborand's meticulous inventory of 1793-1794, preserved in the Yvelines Archives in Versailles, we know not only how Monville had furnished the principal follies, but also the implements in the farm buildings and the animals on the farm. He duly notes a "large, strong draft horse," that Citizen Vincent Simon, the caretaker, declared to have been "blind for several years," a grey donkey of indeterminate age, twenty-six chickens and eight ducks.

Corborand also recorded the names of the species of the plants in the greenhouses and the Orangery. The purpose of the Orangery was to protect tropical trees and shrubs against winter frosts. Among the plants inventoried in the Orangery were sixty orange trees, twenty-three oleanders, nine lemon-scented jasmines from Madeira, four Malabar nut plants, twenty-two strawberry trees and five tomato vines.

In his passion for farming, Monville was certainly motivated by the spirit of physiocracy, an economic theory that reached the apogee of its popularity during the last half of the 18th century. The physiocrats, among them Pierre Samuel du Pont de Nemours (1730-1817), disliked cities and believed that the wealth of nations was derived solely from the value of land and agriculture. Thus, to a large extent, Monville could reside comfortably at the Désert de Retz in a state of virtual autarky, producing most of the necessities of life on the premises.

Nothing remains of Monville's Obelisk, allegedly made of painted metal sheets attached to a framework. Jean-Marcel Humbert, in *Egyptomania*, writes, "The obelisk…became a feature in the

Théodore Brongniart (1739-1813),[109] to compete for the design of a ruined pyramid for his park at Mauperthuis, near the town of Coulommiers, east of Paris. Brongniart won the competition, and his pyramid was depicted in a painting by the landscape artist Claude-Louis Châtelet (1753-1795).[110] Both of these pyramids were used for Masonic ceremonies and had an entrance at ground level, permitting easy access. However, as indicated previously, there is no solid evidence that François Racine de Monville belonged to any Masonic lodge, and his membership in the Knights of Noble Archery is this author's speculation.

From the 17th to the 19th century, blocks of ice were harvested from frozen freshwater lakes and streams and delivered to retailers in the towns and to private citizens wealthy enough to possess the space and the means to construct underground icehouses. Three of the 13 icehouses that Louis XIV constructed at Versailles remain today, and four are located on the grounds of the Château of Chantilly.[111] Unlike the Masonic pyramids of Monceau and Mauperthuis, the entrance to Monville's pyramid opened to a 6-meter (18-foot) drop straight down. The interior is a

---

[109] Brongniart designed the Paris stock exchange—the Bourse—known as the Palais Brongniart.

[110] The pyramid at Mauperthuis is still standing, but the site is closed to the public. Châtelet's works hangs in a private collection.

[111] The illuminated interior of the underground icehouse at the Propriété Caillebotte in Yerres, southeast of Paris, constructed in 1830 by Pierre Frédéric Borrel beneath an artificial grotto, can be viewed from an observation platform.

111

huge chamber where the ice was stored in layers separated by straw. A sump at the bottom of the chamber allowed water from the melting ice to be evacuated. In the summer months, ice was removed and used to chill drinks and prepare sherbets. Foodstuffs could also be packed into containers and preserved in the icehouses.

It is therefore obvious that Monville simply intended the pyramid to symbolize ancient Egypt in his microcosm—not forgetting that its primary purposes were to store ice and prevent perishable provisions from spoiling. In 1791-1792, an almost identical pyramid icehouse, designed by Karl Gotthard Langhans, was built in the New Garden in Potsdam, Germany.

Because of its solid construction, and thanks to careful restoration, the Pyramid Icehouse remains today the building that is most faithful to its original design.

The Rockery (sometimes inaccurately described as a grotto), located just inside the principal entrance to the Désert de Retz from the Forêt de Marly, was completed in 1781. Outside, massive, almost megalithic, rusticated blocks guarded the portal. Inside, striding a chaos of artificially-designed stones, statues of satyrs brandishing burning torches lit the visitor's way into Monville's microcosm.

A mentioned previously, the *Mémoires Secrets*

report that Marie Antoinette made numerous visits to Monsieur de Monville's Desert, where she drew inspiration for the construction of her own picturesque garden, the Queen's Hamlet at Trianon. One account has it that she arrived at the Desert accompanied by her lady-in-waiting, Princess Marie-Thérèse de Lamballe, and a retinue of courtiers, and requested of Monville the kindness of a bowl of milk. Monville promptly complied, offering the queen fresh warm milk from one of the cows in his herd, adding, "Where does Your Majesty wish to be served?" "Just here, on the steps of the Temple of Love," by which she was referring to the Temple of Pan.

The Princesse de Lamballe (1749-1792) was one of the most compelling of Monville's contemporaries. Born into the House of Savoy, she was eighteen when she married the fabulously wealthy Prince de Lamballe, in 1767. After her husband died a year later, "exhausted from a life of debauchery," she became a confidante of Marie Antoinette. Subsequently, she left the court and became involved in the Masonic movement. She was inducted into a women's lodge known as La Candeur on February 12, 1777, and on January 10, 1781, she was elected Grand Mistress of the Scottish Mother Lodge. Like Olympe de Gouges, the Princess de Lamballe, was a feminist before her time and shocked the court and irritated the queen by organizing a dinner followed by a ball to which only women were invited.

113

Due to her close connection with Marie Antoinette,[112] she was arrested on August 10, 1792, and, because she refused to "take an oath to love liberty and equality and to swear hatred to the king and the queen and to the monarchy," she was delivered to a mob and dismembered on September 3, 1792.

On March 24, 1783, after extensive negotiations, Monsieur de Monville succeeded in leasing the ruined Gothic church of Saint-Jacques-et-Saint-Christophe from the Premonstratensian monks of the nearby Priory of Joyenval.[113] The ruins, dating from the 13th or 14th century, remained Church property until they were expropriated during the French Revolution.

One can pose the question as to why Monville was so eager to take possession of a ruined parish church. Once again, the answer may lie in Monville's conception of the Désert de Retz as a microcosm. The ruined church—the only real ruin in the garden—was an obvious symbol of the decline of Christianity, particularly that of the Roman Catholic Church, during the Age of Enlightenment. The dechristianization of France would culminate just six years later in the

---

[112] Scurrilous pamphlets illustrated with crude pornographic drawings depicting the princess engaging in "lesbian orgies" with Marie Antoinette and others were circulated at the time.

[113] Legend has it that Queen Clotilde (465-545), widow of Clovis (465-511), the first king of France, retired to a hermitage at Joyenval.

confiscation of Church property, the execution of many clerics and the destruction or disfiguring of many churches or their conversion into Temples of the Goddess Reason. On November 10, 1793 (20 Brumaire II), the old Christian altar of Notre Dame de Paris was dismantled and replaced by a new one dedicated to Liberty, and "To Philosophy" was inscribed over the cathedral's doors. Religion in France was officially dead.

Starting in 1782, Monville was able to spend time in the Column House, without doubt one of the most bizarre and arresting residences in the history of architecture, one of the rare examples of visionary architecture to be realized. The Column House is so unusual that in 2007 it was included in a list of the "Top Seven Weirdest Houses in the World."[114]

The English critic and author Cyril Connolly devotes one chapter in his book, *Les Pavillons: French Pavilions of the Eighteenth Century*, to the Désert de Retz. Connolly writes:

> The little park and everything in it are a splendid hymn to ruin, an elegy on dead fashion, the main building is one of the most beautiful and original designs for living one could imagine, a perfect merger

---

[114] The others are the Hundertwasser Haus in Vienna, Austria; the Upside-down House in Szymbark, Poland; Haewoojae--the Toilet-Shaped House—in Suwon, South Korea; the House on the Stick in Portland, OR, and the Glass House in New Canaan, CT.

of classical with romantic.[115]

Connolly quotes the prolific historian of French chateaux and gardens, Count Ernest de Ganay (1880-1963), who considered Monville's Column House "the most interesting building of the eighteenth century."

The Column House is a four-story false ruin in the shape of a monumental, truncated Doric column that stands 80 feet (25 meters) high and 50 feet (15 meters) in diameter. Not only was the column voluntarily incomplete—the "complete" column would have stretched 360 feet (over a hundred meters) into the sky—but Monville's unique design included artificial cracks and fissures in the exterior walls.

Both Thomas Blaikie and Charles Joseph, Prince de Ligne, the author of a widely-read treatise on picturesque gardens, *Coup d'œil sur Belœil,* interpreted the "destroyed column" as symbolic of the Tower of Babel, from whence God "did there confound the language of all the earth." Swedish art historian Magnus Olausson[116] suggests that "the broken column was meant to be a Masonic allegory." The column also serves as a metaphor for the shattered remnants of the glorious Roman

---

[115] Connolly, Cyril and Zerbe, Jerome, *Les Pavillons*, New York, Macmillan, 1962.
[116] In "Freemasonry, Occultism and the Picturesque Garden towards the End of the Eighteenth Century," *Art History*, 1985.

Empire, the once mighty civilization reduced to rubble.[117]

The four floors of the Column House, with four rooms on each, are connected by a spiral staircase in a circular stair hall. Windows were placed in the flutes of the column. As architectural historian Robert Rosenblum wrote in *Transformations in Late Eighteenth Century Art*, the building was, "not only fenestrated but actually contained four stories of highly specialized rooms that permitted aristocratic habitation of, and therefore the most intense empathy with, a fictional relic of a classical past."

The interior space was divided into rooms in the shapes of ovals, circles, semiovals and semicircles. Although the rooms were small, judicially placed mirrors gave the illusion that the rooms were much larger. The glass skylight on the roof allowed sunlight to flood the stairwell, bringing the outdoors indoors. The spiral staircase continued the theme; pots of flowers—carnations, periwinkles, arum lilies and heliotropes—were hung along its length.

The attic was reserved for Monville's laboratory, a studio—where he kept a forge and a cabinetmaker's bench—and a hydraulic device that pumped water into a reservoir for the lavatories.

Two small round water colors—artist unknown—

---

[117] Hubert Robert designed a Ruined Gothic Tower for the park at Betz that is still standing.

dating from the late 18th century were purchased at auction by the town of Chambourcy in April 2012. One depicts the Chinese House and the Temple of Pan. The other shows the Column House surrounded by what appears to be a moat, crossed by a rustic footbridge. Plates four and nine in Le Rouge's Cahier XIII show the bridge but not the moat.

Another unique feature of Monsieur de Monville's Column House is that it is likely to have been one of the earliest buildings in France to be equipped with a lightning rod. True to his innovative nature, Monville appears to have been one of the first adopters in France of the new technology.

Benjamin Franklin's experiments with electricity led him to design the world's first lightning rod in 1752. News of Franklin's experience soon reached Europe. During a trip to Europe in 1767, accompanied by his frequent traveling companion, the Scots physician Sir John Pringle (1707-1782), Franklin met with a number of influential French scientists and politicians and was introduced to Louis XV. One of the scientists, Thomas-François Dalibard (1709-1778), had replicated Franklin's experiment with lightning in May 1752 at Marly-la-Ville and, it is reported, befriended Franklin.

A plaque on the building occupying the site of the Hôtel de Valentinois in Passy, where Franklin and his grandsons lived from December 1777 to 1785, erroneously states that he had installed the first lightning rod in France on the building. In fact, the first known lightning rods in France were mounted on the Hôtel de l'Académie and the Church of Saint-Philibert in Dijon in 1776. It is known, however, that Franklin supervised the installation of a lightning rod on the Church of Saint-Clément in Arpajon in 1782.

However, these devices were not met with universal approval, and opposition arose due to the fact that some were improperly installed, resulting in accidental lightning strikes. In 1783, Charles Dominique de Visséry de Bois-Valé (?-1784), an amateur scientist in the town of Saint-Omer, was sued by his neighbors who wanted him to dismantle the lightning rod he had installed on his chimney in 1780, fearing it might set fire to the whole neighborhood. The trial was held in the town of Arras and the defendant was represented by Maximilien Robespierre, then only 25 years old, who based his defense on scientific theories. Judgment was rendered on May 14, 1783, in favor of de Visséry. It was considered a precedent-setting victory of science over superstition and launched the career of the young lawyer from Arras. [118]

Monville's Column House was completed in 1781. Carmontelle 's *Vue perspective du Désert de Retz,* in the collection of the National Museum in Stockholm, dating from 1785, as well as the 1808 Constant Bourgeois rendering of the Column House

---

[118] Jessica Rivkin has written a thorough description of the trial in an essay, "The Lawyer and the Lightning Rod," in *Science in Context* 12 1 (1999).

and the Chambourcy watercolor all clearly show a vertical mast, almost certainly a lightning rod, extending above the roof of the Column House.[119]

In 1784, in a treatise entitled *Dell'utilità dei conduttori elettrici,* Italian scientist and inventor Marsilio Landriani published an inventory of all the known lightning rods on private and public buildings in Italy and elsewhere in Europe. Landriani's book illustrates how widespread the use of lightning rods had become in the mere thirty years since Franklin had unveiled his invention.

Of the 35 lightning rods inventoried in France, eleven were in Paris and one in suburban Châtillon on the residence of Adrienne-Catherine de Noailles, Madame de Tessé (1741-1813), a friend of Thomas Jefferson. Landriani catalogued many others in Bordeaux, Bourg-en-Bresse, Chantilly, Dijon, (including the two cited above), Lyons, Montbard and Orléans, as well as Visséry de Bois-Valé's in Saint-Omer.

Consequently, if there was indeed a lightning rod on the Column House, it would either have been installed after 1784, or it would have escaped Landriani's attention because of its remote location.

Corborand's inventory of Monsieur de Monville's library allows us to discover its owner's taste in literature. Among the collection was a seven-tome

---

[119] The Carmontelle work is reproduced in books about the Désert de Retz by Cendres and Radiguet and Diana Ketcham.

encyclopedia of poetry, an eleven-volume set of the universal history of theater and a *Dictionnaire de la Musique* by Rousseau, published in 1768.

As one would expect, Monville's library contained numerous works relating to gardening and horticulture; it is reported that Marie Antoinette consulted them during her visits. Among the books were a set of 48 comprising the *Bibliothèque de la Campagne*, *Le Gentilhomme Cultivateur* in 16 volumes, and a dictionary of plants.

Some of the other books showing Monville's wide interests were *La Paysanne Pervertie* by the prolific Rétif de la Bretonne (1734-1806), the poetry of Horace and, most bizarre of all, *Le Cousin de Mahomet* a novel by Nicolas Fromaget (?-1759), in which a French schoolboy leaves Paris in a convoy of convicts and ends up with no more than a whistle as a slave in an Ottoman harem in Constantinople where he falls in love with the beautiful Nédoüa, a descendant of the Prophet Mohammed—hence the title. Written in 1742 and immediately banned, the book has been periodically reissued and is still in print. It was described in 2007 by French author and critic Jean d'Ormesson as "an authentic manifesto of the French Enlightenment" and "an exotic, orientalist, picaresque and libertine adventure."

A fifth level, a cellar, was connected to the kitchen in the commons next door by a tunnel that is still in existence.[120] François Corborand's inventory of the contents of the cellar allows us to discover Monsieur de Monville's taste in libations other than tea, coffee and chocolate. One hundred fifty bottles of "old red Burgundy" and twenty-four bottles of sparkling Champagne were noted, along with smaller quantities of Hermitage, Graves and Canon-Fronsac. Thirty-eight bottles of ale and a keg of hard cider produced in Chambourcy were also found in the cellar. Corborand estimated their total value as 248 *livres*.

Aside from the furniture, Corborand noted some other items of interest inside the Column House. One of those was listed as a walnut *boîte d'optique*, known in English as a peep box. One might consider these devices the 18th century equivalent of television, since they allowed viewers to learn about faraway places and current events and enjoy fantasy scenes by peering through a magnifying lens at intaglio, hand-colored images reflected on a mirror. By exaggerating converging lines, the engraved prints produced an optical illusion of depth.

Other items allowing us to imagine how Monsieur de Monville and his guests passed the time were decks of cards to play piquet, chess and checker sets whose pieces were carved in ivory and ebony, boards to play trictrac (a variant of backgammon), a

---

[120] Le Rouge's engraving of the Column House shows two cellars, lending additional credence to the suggestion that he never actually visited the Désert de Retz, but based his engravings on sketches by others, enhanced by his own imagination.

122

set of numbered balls and 16 playing cards used in a parlor game related to bingo known as loto and a *jeu de solitaire* in walnut where the object was to remove all the pegs save one from the board by jumping one peg over another.

At the moment that Corborand and his colleagues discovered a fortepiano, Citizen Simon declared that the instrument belonged to an architect named Desgranges, living in Boissy St. Leger, and had been lent to the Englishman who had purchased the Désert de Retz in 1792, Lewis Disney-Ffytche, "for the amusement of his daughters."

The bedroom was decorated with paintings by well-known artists. Corborand declared a view of a seaport to be the work Louis Jean-François Lagrenée (1724-1805), but this attribution is doubtful, since Lagrenée chose his subjects from mythology, history and religion. Corborand identified another painting of a seaport as the work of "Van Loo," perhaps without realizing that the Van Loo dynasty included two generations totaling five painters. It is documented elsewhere that Monville owned a still-life, *Fruits et Fleurs*, by Michel-Bruno Bellengé (1726-1793).

Monville's collection also included one of Hubert Robert's two paintings entitled *Le Décintrement du Pont de Neuilly* [121] depicting the moment on

---

[121] The works are now in the collections of the Musée de l'Ile de France in Sceaux and the Musée Carnavalet in Paris.

September 22, 1772, when the scaffolding supporting the arches of the bridge was cast into the Seine in the presence of Louis XV, Madame du Barry and a vast throng of onlookers. [122]

One may legitimately wonder why Monville would have chosen this work for his bedroom. Several reasons come to mind. First of all, between 1774 and 1776, he owned the Petit Château in Neuilly-sur-Seine, within sight of the newly-constructed bridge.

Another reason was Monville's interest in science and technology, particularly architecture. The low-arch bridge at Neuilly, designed by Jean-Rodolphe Perronet was considered a triumph of engineering because of the revolutionary building technique he utilized. Perronet was the first to recognize that for bridges of equal spans, the intermediate piers carry only vertical loads and can be made quite thin. His bridges were consequently quite light and elegant: the Pont de Neuilly had five arches of a 40-meter (128-foot) span each, yet the piers were only 4 meters (13 feet) thick.

Although Perronet's Pont de Neuilly was dismantled starting in 1936, his Pont de la Concorde in Paris,

---

[122] On March 10, 1811, the remainder of Monville's personal effects at the Désert de Retz were auctioned. Hubert Robert's canvas fetched 50 francs and the purported Van Loo and Lagrenée works were sold as one lot for 60 francs.

utilizing the same technique[123] and completed in 1791, remains standing, as do his bridges in the towns of Brunoy and Nemours.

Finally, the biography of the great architect would have certainly intrigued Monville. Perronet's father, David, was a young cadet in the Swiss Guards, and his mother, Marie Travers, was a 19-year old *vigneronne*; her father owned vineyards on the slopes of Mont Valérien in the Paris suburb of Suresnes, the town where Perronet was born. Winemaking in the area around Paris reached its apogee in the 18th century, and vineyards extending over more than 42,000 hectares (103,000 acres) made it the largest wine-producing region in France. The slopes of Mont Valérien were covered with vineyards until the epidemic of phylloxera parasites in the late 19th century wrought havoc on most of the vineyards in France.[124]

Perronet's future seemed anything but auspicious because his parents weren't married and—worse— his father was Protestant at a time when most Protestants were second-class citizens. After the murder of his father in 1725, the 17-year old Perronet was hired as an apprentice draftsman in an architectural firm in Paris. His subsequent rise to

---

[123] Cut stones recovered from the ruins of the Bastille were utilized in its construction.

[124] Five thousand bottles of chardonnay per year are still produced in the Clos du Pas Saint-Maurice in Suresnes and sold to the public.

fame was spectacular: he became chief engineer to Louis XV, laid out a network of roads and designed twenty bridges throughout the kingdom. Elected to membership in numerous learned societies, Perronet's career culminated in 1747 when he became the first director of the Ecole Nationale des Ponts et Chaussées, the national school of civil engineering, a position he held until his death at the age of 85.

Although Monville's situation was somewhat less precarious than Perronet's, they both succeeded despite many obstacles. Both lost their fathers early in their lives: Monville was virtually orphaned at the age of eight, and when Perronet was just seventeen, his father was murdered. Monville might have seen in Perronet a kindred spirit, another luminary who rose to prominence despite the odds.

Intriguingly, in a small vestibule on the second floor of the Column House, Corborand catalogued "two family portraits in their wooden frames." We will never know if they were portraits of Monville and his relatives or of the Disney-Ffytche family.

Bronzes and figures in Sèvres porcelain were placed on mantels and tables in the Column House. The walls and much of the furniture were covered in Toile de Jouy, a decorative cotton cloth imprinted in monochrome and produced in a factory located in the town of Jouy-en-Josas, near Versailles, founded in 1760 by Christophe-Philippe Oberkampf (1738-

1815). Typical motifs depicted pastoral scenes or evoke rural life or historic events.[125]

Following Corborand's exhaustive inventory—he even noted six toothbrushes—everything on the premises was confiscated except for some articles Corborand judged to be reminders of royalty. These included nine statuettes discovered outside the Chinese House, believed by Corborand to be representations of kings, but which were most likely the Nine Muses draped in their abollas. Corborand, ever the fervent revolutionary, smashed these idols on the spot. Some articles made of copper were earmarked for the army. Bedding and linens were reserved for military hospitals, and several of the rarest plants were transferred to the Jardin des Plantes, the principal botanical garden in France. The remaining personal effects were sold at auction.

François Racine de Monville, who manifested an intense curiosity in science throughout his life, was one of many whose imagination was captured by flying machines and lighter-than-air balloons; in fact, the Désert de Retz was destined to become a cradle of French aviation.

In mid-August 1781, the Désert de Retz was the site of the assembly and testing of one of the world's earliest aircraft, the *Vaisseau-Volant* or Flying Vessel, the brainchild of a self-educated inventor

---

[125] Modern versions of Toile de Jouy are still produced.

named Jean-Pierre Blanchard (1753-1809), who, like Monville, was a Norman, born and raised in the historic town of Les Andelys, only 6.2 kilometers (3.8 miles) from Monville's ancestral property at Le Thuit.

Blanchard, a mechanical genius, had designed and built automata and hydraulic pumps in his youth. The historian Edouard Pelay, in an article on Blanchard published in 1899, notes that Blanchard's first invention was a rattrap that dispatched its victims with a self-inflicted shot from a pistol. At the age of sixteen, he designed a pedal-powered *voiture mechanique* and drove it the 40 kilometers (25 miles) between Les Andelys and Rouen.

It was only natural that Blanchard would soon turn his attention to the possibilities of human flight, and the best account of his research and development can be found in Jules Duhem's *Histoire des Idées Aéronautiques avant Montgolfier*, published in Paris in 1943. Inspired by the Andean condor (*Vultur gryphus*), Blanchard's Flying Vessel was basically a human-powered ornithopter, a heavier-than-air craft designed to be propelled through the air by flapping its wings. The Flying Vessel's pilot, seated in an enclosed cabin spacious enough to accommodate a passenger seated in tandem, utilized a system of levers, pedals and pulleys to propel the craft both vertically and horizontally by flapping its six wings, with direction controlled by a rudder.

Duhem states that Blanchard constructed his flying

machine "chez M. de Monville" and tested it on August 28, 1781, "dans le domaine de M. de Monville." [126] Blanchard described the *Vaisseau-Volant* in letters published in the *Journal de Paris*, on pages 966-967 of the issue of August 28 and page 1160 of the issue of October 25, 1781. He stated that he had been working on the project for twelve years, but had chosen the location "near Saint-Germain-en-Laye" since its isolation enabled him to construct his flying vessel in secret. Blanchard wrote in 1784 that he had used a *moulinet*—his term for an air screw or propeller—placed horizontally over his head, to help him leap from the ground: "This I performed, in the year 1781, at Mr. Monville's, near Saint- Germain-en-Laye." [127]

It is also likely that Monville subsidized the project, at least partially, since Blanchard, the son of a metal worker, was not a man of means. Realizing that he would need to protect his face while aloft, Blanchard also designed what may have been the world's first flight helmet. [128]

According to Edouard Pelay, "Throngs of the curious, including the brothers of Louis XVI, the Duc de Chartres, the Duc de Bourbon and other

---

[126] Duhem, pages 174, 279.

[127] *Journal and Certificates on the Fourth Voyage of Mr. Blanchard,* London, 1784, note, page 3.

[128] A color cutaway view of the craft engraved by Blanchard's friend, the ornithologist François-Nicolas Martinet (c. 1760-1800) in the Bibliothèque Nationale de France can be viewed on Gallica.

dignitaries," flocked to the Désert de Retz to inspect Blanchard's flying machine.[129] Blanchard stated on August 28 that these "Grands seigneurs" had promised him a substantial reward should the project succeed. After his preliminary experiments at the Désert de Retz, Blanchard scheduled a public test flight in Paris for May 5, 1782. Before a huge crowd of spectators, the Flying Vessel was unable to leave the ground, and Blanchard became the laughing stock of Paris.

The next year, on June 4, 1783, the Montgolfier brothers, Joseph Michel and Jacques-Etienne, flew an unmanned hot-air balloon named *Séraphina* in a demonstration in Annonay, 70 km (43 miles) south of Lyons. The flight covered two kilometers (1.2 miles), lasted 10 minutes, and attained an estimated altitude of 1,600-2,000 meters (5,200-6,600 feet). The news traveled fast, and on August 26, 1783, Jacques Charles (1746-1823) launched the first hydrogen-filled balloon from the Champs de Mars in Paris; among the spectators was Benjamin Franklin.

In October of 1783, Monville is reported to have utilized an aerostat or tethered balloon as a method of communicating with his employees living in the nearby village of Saint-Nom-la-Bretèche.[130]

---

[129] "Pierre Blanchard, aéronaute; histoire de ses ascensions," in *Bulletin des amis des monuments rouennais*, 1899.

[130] Aerostats are used today for both civilian and military purposes.

Jean-François Pilâtre de Rozier (1754-1785) and the Marquis François Laurent d'Arlandes (1742-1809) became the world's first aviation pioneers on November 21, 1783, when they took off in a Montgolfier balloon from the Bois de Boulogne and landed 25 minutes later on the Butte aux Cailles, in the present-day Thirteenth Arrondissement of Paris, after reaching an estimated altitude of 1,000 meters (3,000 feet).

Meanwhile, Jean-Pierre Blanchard, undaunted by the embarrassing failure of his Flying Vessel in 1782, promptly adopted balloon flight after the successful demonstration of the Montgolfiers and, following his first flight on March 2, 1784, began barnstorming throughout the Continent and England.[131] On January 7, 1785, Blanchard and his American co-pilot, Dr. John Jeffries (1744-1819), a physician and scientist, who had underwritten the project with an investment of 100 golden guineas, completed the first successful flight across the Channel, using a hydrogen-filled balloon. Taking advantage of a tailwind provided by the Prevailing Westerlies, in just two hours and twenty minutes the adventurous duo flew from Dover to Guînes, whose citizens subsequently erected a column to commemorate their exploit. A few months later, on June 15, 1785, Pilâtre de Rozier attempted the crossing from east to west in his *Rozière*, but crashed and died in the French seaside town of

---

[131] Blanchard fitted a small, six-bladed, hand-rotated *moulinet* to the car of a balloon he flew in London on October 16, 1784, to provide forward movement.

Wimereux shortly after takeoff. [132]

After crossing the Atlantic, Blanchard conducted the first hot-air balloon flight in the Western Hemisphere on January 9, 1793, taking off from Philadelphia and landing in Deptford Township, NJ. President George Washington, as well as the next four presidents, John Adams, Thomas Jefferson, James Madison and James Monroe, witnessed Blanchard's pioneering flight. According to his journal, [133] he conducted a number of scientific experiments while airborne and was kept company by his "trusty companion, a little black dog." In one of these tests, Blanchard recorded that a magnet that had been able to raise a weight of 5 ounces Avoirdupois (141 grams) on the ground could barely lift 4 ounces (113 grams) at an altitude of 5,812 feet (1,771 meters).

Upon his return to France in 1797, Blanchard continued piloting hot-air balloons and died on March 7, 1809, as a result of a sixty-foot (twenty meter) fall that occurred during his 66th flight, near The Hague, in the Netherlands, when he suffered a stroke and was unable to maintain the fire in his balloon's burner.

Jean-Pierre Blanchard having died a debtor, his

---

[132] The aeronauts flew three types of balloons: the *Montgolfière* was filled with hot air, the *Charlière* used hydrogen and the *Rozière* was a hybrid, with separate chambers for the two gases.

[133] "Journal of my Forty-Fifth Ascension...," first published in 1793 and reprinted in 1918 and in facsimile in 2010.

second wife, *née* Marie Madeleine-Sophie Armant (1778-1819), who had accompanied her husband, flying dual, as early as 1805, began her own career, piloting her *Charlières* solo in a total of 67 ascents across Europe and garnering many honors, including that of "Aeronaut of the Official Festivals," presented to her by Napoleon Bonaparte.

It can be said that Sophie Blanchard, as she was known, was even more intrepid than her late husband. On her way to Rome in 1811, her balloon attained an altitude of 3,600 meters (11,800 feet); on another occasion, she blacked out at high altitude in a flight that lasted over fourteen hours, and on a trip to Turin on April 26, 1812, the temperature dropped so low that she suffered a nosebleed and ice formed on her hands and face. Sophie risked her life by adding daredevil stunts such as shooting off fireworks while airborne to the program of her one-woman air shows. On July 6, 1819, Sophie Blanchard lost her life in a fiery crash following one of her pyrotechnic displays when her hydrogen-filled balloon caught fire over the Tivoli Gardens in Paris. [134] It was eerie portent of the *Hindenburg* disaster of May 6, 1937, in which the hydrogen-filled zeppelin caught fire and crashed at Lakehurst, NJ, resulting in 36 fatalities among the 97 passengers and crew.

---

[134] The Tivoli Gardens occupied the site of the present-day Gare Saint-Lazare in the Eighth Arrondissement.

On June 4, 1784, in Lyons, Elisabeth Thible, an opera singer, became the world's first aviatrix. Costumed as Minerva, she ascended in a balloon named *La Gustave*, in honor of King Gustav III of Sweden, who was visiting the city on his way from Italy to Paris. During the 45-minute flight, she sang duos from a popular opera by Pierre-Alexandre Monsigny, *La belle Arsène*, with her fellow aeronaut, a Monsieur Fleurant. Another early aviation pioneer, André-Jacques Garnerin, performed the world's first successful parachute jump in the Parc Monceau in Paris on October 22, 1797 (1 Brumaire V). On October 12, 1799, his student and future wife, Jeanne Geneviève Labrosse, became the first woman skydiver. Due to his interest in scientific innovation, Monville might have experimented with other methods of contacting his employees besides the aerostat. It is possible that he used a system utilizing metal tubes to communicate over long distances similar to the Acoustic Telegraph, invented by a 25-year old Cistercian monk, Dom Gauthey (1742-1809), in 1782. Gauthey presented his invention to the French Academy of Sciences in Paris where it caught the attention of Condorcet, who evaluated it in a report. A subscription was launched in order to finance a trial over a short distance. Subscribers included the astronomer Jérôme Lalande, Pilâtre de Rozier, the mathematician Antoine Deparcieux, Benjamin Franklin and the radical journalist and politician Jean-Paul Marat. [135] The experiment, directed by

---

[135] Marat was a political extremist and the publisher of *L'Ami du Peuple*. He

Condorcet, was successfully conducted in 1782 in Paris over a distance of 800 meters (a little over 2,600 feet). Unable to find additional investors to develop his system in France, Dom Gauthey left for America in order to seek financial support. He published a 32-page prospectus in Philadelphia in 1783, but his fund-raising efforts were unsuccessful.

Certainly, Monsieur de Monville would have followed with interest developments in long-distance aerial communication. A flag semaphore system known as the Aerial Telegraph was developed by Bernard Thomas Tréhouart (1754-1804) and tested in June 1794. A series of towers was projected to link Paris and Brest—one such tower was located in Chambourcy—and messages were transmitted using flags and pennants similar to the signal flags still used during underway replenishment at sea. In March 1796 the experiment was abandoned.

A more successful semaphore telegraph system, known as the Optical Telegraph, was first tested in 1791 by Claude Chappe (1763-1805) and his four brothers and became operational in 1794. Their system consisted of a series of towers, each equipped with two arms connected by a cross-arm. The arms had seven positions, and the cross-arm had four more permitting a 196-combination code. The

---

was stabbed to death in his copper-lined bathtub by a political opponent, Charlotte Corday, who was, in turn, executed on the guillotine. Marat's death was immortalized by the painter Jacques-Louis David.

arms were from three to thirty feet long, painted black, and counterweighted, moved by only two handles.

The first line was constructed between Paris and Lille, with 55 relay towers from 12 to 25 km (10 to 20 miles) apart. The Paris tower was located on the highest point in Paris—128 meters above sea level—near today's appropriately named Télégraphe Metro station. Short, coded messages could be transmitted over the 220 kilometers (136 miles) between the two cities in approximately half an hour. The Chappe network was extended throughout the country and used until 1855. One of the towers, dating from 1798, is located in Marly-le-Roi, not far from Chambourcy, and has been restored.

After traveling through Italy and witnessing in Lyons the ascension of Madame Thible in the *montgolfière* named in his honor, King Gustav III arrived in Paris on June 7, 1784, for a visit of six weeks. Although previously reported that Gustav stayed at the Désert de Retz as Monsieur de Monville's guest, recent research has revealed that the king only visited Monville's garden on July 14, 1784. We can be certain that lighter-than-air balloon flight was one of the subjects the king discussed with his host.

On the evening of Monday, June 21, 1784, Queen Marie Antoinette organized an elaborate celebration with fireworks, music and dancing—a *fête de nuit*—

at the Petit Trianon in honor of King Gustav. Since Monville was friendly with the queen and with Gustav, whom he had received the previous week, it is possible if not likely that he attended the event.

The king was so impressed with Monville's Désert that he promptly contacted him requesting the plans of the garden. Monville responded favorably, and the documents, archived in Sweden, served as an inspiration for Gustav's English Garden in the grounds at Drottningholm and the buildings in Hagaparken. Gustav entrusted his ambassador, Erik Magnus Staël von Holstein, to send Monville a gold box encrusted with diamonds outlining the royal monogram as a token of his appreciation.

In 2014, Magnus Olausson published an article[136] illustrated by reproductions of the documents that Monville sent to Gustav in 1785. Among those is a large-size (1.5 by 2.25 meter) General Plan of the Désert in watercolors, most likely executed by Monville himself, discovered in the Nordiska museet in Stockholm, depicting buildings, garden ornaments and plantings. On each side are unique color views of ten *fabriques* shown as framed paintings and arranged vertically: on the left are the Chinese House, the Rockery, the Temple of Pan, the Open-air Theater and the Tomb. To the right are the Orangery, the Pyramid Icehouse, the Hermitage, the Dairy and the Temple of Repose. Olausson cites

---

[136] "The Désert de Retz Revisited," in *Art Bulletin of Nationalmuseum Stockholm*, Volume 21, Stockholm, 2014.

numerous differences between the park as depicted in Monville's General Plan and in the Le Rouge engravings. For example, the Obelisk is placed next to the Rockery Entrance in the General Plan, but Le Rouge places it near the kitchen garden.

Olausson concludes, "All these discrepancies show that the park had yet to find its definitive shape, and that Monville was constantly refashioning and extending his project. The general plan which [Monville] sent to the Swedish king was, therefore, not a record of what had actually been created, but a mix of features, both existing and envisaged." Unfortunately, Gustav was only able to enjoy his gardens for a short period. His attempts to unite numerous European sovereigns to oppose the French Revolution were unsuccessful and resulted in a conspiracy among his domestic enemies. He was shot in the back by a conspirator named Anckarström on March 16, 1792, at a masked ball and died on March 29 of that year.[137]

Frannçois Corborand's inventory, conducted in December 1793 and January 1794, confirms that Monville possessed an extensive library. It is therefore warranted to speculate about Monville's own literary endeavors.

---

[137] The event inspired Verdi's opera *Un ballo in maschera*.

In an essay,[138] Robert Darnton demonstrates that the late eighteenth century was a time of an outpouring of writing; diaries and memoirs by many of Monville's friends and acquaintances such as Dufort de Cheverny, Alexandre de Tilly and Madame de Genlis were published after their death and widely circulated.

Additionally, many of the owners of the French folly gardens published books describing their creations and articulating their aesthetic theories. The Marquis René-Louis de Girardin, who created one of the first French landscape gardens at Ermenonville, published the influential *De la composition des paysages* in 1777, and in 1786, the Prince de Ligne wrote a treatise entitled *Coup d'oeil sur Beloeil et sur une grande partie des jardins de l'Europe*, in which he praises several of the buildings at the Désert de Retz. "God would be jealous," he writes, of the Column House. He continues, "The Emperor of China would admire the Chinese House, the fruit of the owner's research. At one corner, a rivulet flows out of a grotesque metal mouth and contiues as a pretty stream around two small islands and over several terraced cascades beside a small yet charming formal garden."

In Monville's case, however, aside from the songbooks mentioned previously and a few letters and legal documents bearing his signature, nothing

---

138 Darnton, Robert, "Paris: The Early Internet," in *New York Review of Books*, June 29, 2000.

has surfaced. It is difficult to believe that Monville did not write more than a handful of songs. Certainly someone who was capable of writing musical scores was equally capable of writing articulate French prose! As Diana Ketcham put it, "It is curious that a man with his aesthetic drive left no literary legacy."

It is possible, however, that Monville did keep a journal or set down his theories about landscape architecture, as had many of his contemporaries, or even drafted his memoirs while imprisoned, as had Madame Roland. If he did so, the documents were most likely dispersed or discarded at the time the Désert de Retz and the Hôtels de Monville were sold in 1792 and sequestered by the Revolutionary Government in 1793, or at Monville's death in 1797.

In July 1785, Monville drafted a map of the Désert de Retz, identifying 17 *fabriques* in his estate (see the table below). The same year, Georges-Louis Le Rouge, published a series of 24 engravings of the Désert de Retz in Cahier XIII[139] of his *Cahiers des Jardins Anglo-Chinois*. This document remains the best source of illustrations of the various structures at the Désert de Retz. Due to numerous errors and embellishments in the engravings, however, it is uncertain that Le Rouge set foot in Monville's garden, relying instead on others' sketches and

---

[139] Cahier XIII has been reproduced *in extenso* in the books about the Désert de Retz by Cendres and Radiguet and Diana Ketcham. All 21 volumes may be consulted on Gallica.

descriptions and giving free rein to the caprices of his imagination.

Fabriques in the Désert de Retz in 1785	
Column House	Rockery, Entrance to the Garden
Temple of Pan	Ruined Gothic Church
Chinese House	Dairy
Tenant Farmhouse	Hermitage
Orangery	Island of Happiness
Hothouses	Thatched Hut
Tomb	Pyramid Icehouse
Obelisk	Commons
Open-air Theater	

The Column House, the Temple of Pan, the ruined Gothic Church of Saint-Jacques-et-Saint-Christophe, the Tartar Tent on the Island of Happiness, the Pyramid Icehouse, the Open-air Theater, the Temple of Repose and the Little Altar all exist today in various states of preservation. The Rockery Entrance, the Chinese House, the Dairy, the Hermitage, the Orangery, the Thatched Cottage, the Tomb and the Obelisk, as well as the greenhouses and the farm buildings, have disappeared.

According to historian William Howard Adams,[140] Monville's Open-air Theater, cradled by alignments of stately elm trees, was similar in design to the

---

[140] Adams, William Howard, *The French Garden 1500-1800*, New York, George Braziller, 1979.

141

theater at the Château d'Abondant not far from Anet, in Normandy, built in the 1750's by Nicolas Michot (1707-1790). Michot's theater was enclosed by palisades of green hedge and trimmed banks of hornbeam. [141] Writing about Monville's theater, Adams observes:

> At the Désert, the scene projecting into the garden was composed as a corner of nature where large trees flaunted their branches over the playing area as living stage sets, while trying to conceal their theatrical function and become part of a garden composition.

During the *belle saison*, the Open-air Theater was the scene of plays, ballets and recitals of music by popular composers such as Gluck and his arch-rival Niccolò Vito Piccinni (1728-1800). Both had written operas based on the tragedy *Iphigenia in Tauris* by Euripides that had divided music-lovers into two camps, the Gluckists (Monville among them) and the Piccinnists. The host himself doubtlessly joined his fellow musicians, performing on the harp, the flute or other instruments.

A likely visitor to the Open-air Theater and the Grand Hôtel de Monville was Joseph Bologne, Chevalier de Saint-George, another probable acquaintance of Monville. The two had much in common. If Monville was acclaimed as the best

---

[141] Marie Antoinette, who enjoyed the theater and did not not hesitate to take the stage herself, requested her head gardener, Antoine Richard (1735-1807), in 1774, to draw up the plans of a similar open-air theater for Trianon, but the projecect dwas never executed.

archer in Europe, the Chevalier de Saint-George was considered Europe's best swordsman. Both were outstanding equestrians whose feats elicited praise from their contemporaries, and both were excellent musicians; Saint-George on the violin, Monville on the harp and flute. And both were friends of America.

Joseph Bologne was born on Christmas Day, 1745, on the island of Guadeloupe to Nanon, a freed slave of Senegalese origin, and a white French plantation owner, Georges Bologne de Saint-George. The renowned fencing master Henry Angelo (1716-1802)[142] claimed that Nanon was "one of the most beautiful women that Africa has ever sent to the plantations" and that Joseph "combined in his person his mother's grace and good looks and his father's vigor and assurance." Joseph's father brought him and his mother to France in 1753 and enrolled his son in a private academy; upon graduation he was accepted into the King's Guards.

The young Joseph Bologne began to study music diligently at an early age. A virtuoso violinist, he eventually became Marie Antoinette's musical adviser. As a favorite at the court, he sat for a portrait by Madame Vigée Le Brun. He also became the conductor of the Concert de la Loge Olympique, the largest orchestra in France, all of whose musicians were Freemasons. The Chevalier de Saint-George himself belonged to the lodge of Les

---

[142] He was born Dominico Angelo Malevolti Tremamondo in Leghorn, Italy.

143

Neuf Sœurs, along with many other luminaries including Benjamin Franklin and John Paul Jones.

Among the featured violinists was Michel Paul Guy de Chabanon, a friend of Monville's in his youth. The orchestra also welcomed women musicians, all of whom were members of La Candeur, the female masonic lodge. James H. Johnson informs us in his book *Listening in Paris: A Cultural History*, that in 1785 300 men and 102 women were members of the Concert de la Loge Olympique.

Saint-George commissioned the series of Parisian symphonies by Haydn. A prolific composer, he produced operas, concertos, ballet and numerous chamber music pieces, especially string quartets, and sonatas for harpsichord. Alain Guedé lists 215 works in his biography of Saint-George, many of which have been recorded. Curiously, his opus G 173 bears the title, *Dans mon cœur agité*...which is also the title of an *ariette* with harp accompaniment written by M. de Monville! Was it collaboration or plagiarism?

It is likely that Monville and Saint-George met through one of their mutual acquaintances. The Duc d'Orléans was Monville's hunting companion and on more than one occasion traveled with Saint-George to London, where the Prince of Wales, the future King George IV, welcomed Saint-George as his special guest and invited him to participate in fencing tournaments. He even fought duels in

London with another well-known French fencer, the Chevalier d'Eon. Both Saint-George and Monville were arrested during the Reign of Terror, but both survived. Saint-George outlived Monville by two years, dying on June 12, 1799.[143]

Monville was also an accomplished singer. One of the few anecdotes revealing Monville's personality appears in the memoirs of Alexandre de Tilly (1764-1816), who was a frequent guest of Monville's, both in Chambourcy and in Paris. Tilly recounts in his memoirs that he was performing an air that Monville had composed and dedicated to a young woman he had idolized in his youth, but Monville became cross and scolded him for singing out of tune.

Tilly was a rake and a scoundrel whose principal occupations appeared to be running up debts and seducing women whom he promptly abandoned: not for nothing was he nicknamed *le beau Tilly*. Armandine Rolland recalled a dinner in late 1792 at which both she and Monville were the guests of Madame de Sainte-Amaranthe. One of the invitees, a Monsieur de Morainville, informed the assembly that Tilly, who had been one of Émilie de Sainte-Amaranthe's many thwarted admirers, had fled to Koblenz[144] to escape a popular uprising against the royal family, whom Tilly had defended in his

---

[143] In December 2001, the Rue de Richepanse in Paris was renamed Rue du Chevalier-de-Saint-George.

[144] Many exiled French aristocrats congregated in Koblenz, where they hatched plans to restore the monarchy.

newspaper articles. Armandine Rolland, who was seated facing Émilie, noted that the news had no effect on the young woman, who had spurned Tilly's overtures, and would have considered the absent Tilly to be "one less among the host of her idolaters." Monville, who was always ready with a witty and sometimes caustic remark, observed tersely as he savored a slice of pineapple, "What will become of all of Tilly's widows?"

One of Tilly's most notorious exploits occurred in 1799, when his peregrinations took him to America. The handsome French nobleman promptly seduced a 15-year old Philadelphian, Maria Matilda Bingham (1783-1849), the stunning, dark-haired daughter of the affluent and prominent Senator William Bingham, President pro tempore of the United States Senate and third in the line of succession to the presidency after the vice president and the speaker of the House of Representatives. Tilly and Miss Bingham eloped and were secretly wed on April 11, 1799; in June, Tilly departed for Europe without his bride, causing great consternation in the Bingham household. The situation was resolved through negotiations; Tilly, represented by a third party, agreed to sign the divorce papers in return for a compensation of 5,000 pounds sterling extorted from Senator Bingham![145] After leading a life of dissipation in England, Germany and Belgium,

---

[145] On April 19, 1802, Maria Matilda married British banker Henry Baring with whom she had five children. After their divorce in 1824, she married the Marquis de Blaisel in Paris on April 17, 1826.

Alexandre de Tilly, unable to pay a gambling debt, committed suicide in Brussels on December 23, 1816. His memoirs were published in 1828.

As can be expected, a singer, instrumentalist and composer such as Monsieur de Monville would have been an ardent opera-lover. We learn from Ernest Boysse (1836-?), the author of *Les Abonnés de l'Opéra (1783 - 1786),* that, for the 1783-1784 season, Monville had purchased a subscription for Box Number 2, which seated four, in the Fourth Balcony *derrière le Paradis*[146] for the sum of 1,500 *livres.* By renting the entire box, Monville could treat his friends and acquaintances to a night at the opera. What makes Boysse's book all the more captivating is that he regales the reader with what he calls *bruits de coulisse*—backstage gossip—and anecdotes about many of the opera patrons, who represented all classes of society and a wide array of professions. [147]

Monville alone merits one of the longest entries, almost four pages, mostly devoted to a somewhat fanciful and dithyrambic evocation of the Désert de Retz, which, like that of the memorialist writing in the *Mémoires Secrets,* evokes a retreat like the Thebaid:

---

[146] In English, the term for these seats is "the gods."

[147] The opera at the Palais Royal having burned on June 8, 1781, performances were given in a temporary location at the Porte-Saint-Martin from October 21, 1781, until July 27, 1794 (9 Thermidor II).

One arrives through an entryway made in imitation of Don Quixote's Cave of Montesinos. Once inside, groves, villages, meadows, streams, bridges, aqueducts, reservoirs, barns, caves, ruins, statues, mazes, flower beds, trellises and all manner of surprises are visible from so many natural viewpoints that the place becomes a veritable fairyland.

Boysse notes that he gleaned much of his information about Monville from Louis André Paulian (1847-1933), a son-in-law of Frédéric Passy (1822-1912); Passy owned the Désert de Retz when Boysse was researching his book.

The Little Altar, described by Monville as *Le Petit autel presque ruiné,* [148] is a small stone column standing between the Column Housee and the Temple of Pan, decorated with garlands and surmounted with a lopsided urn. Although the Little Altar can be easily overlooked or ignored, it may have held greater significance for Monville. His garden had a real ruin, the Gothic Church; an artificial ruin, the Column House; and an altar that was *almost* ruined, as symbolized by the vase that was tipped over, but had not yet fallen to the ground. The Little Altar was also easily visible from the windows of the Column House, permitting Monville and his guests to reflect on the dynamic nature of the universe, that all human endeavor is fleeting, fragile, and ephemeral.

---

[148] "The almost ruined small altar."

Not only styles of architecture were represented in Monsieur de Monville's microcosm, but all the world's principal religions and philosophical systems, from the beliefs of ancient Egypt and those of classical Greece and Rome to Christianity, Confucianism and Islam.

The Tartar Tent on its Island of Happiness can be understood as an evocation of Islam. Tartary was the name used in Europe until the 20th century to designate the great steppes of northern and central Asia, inhabited by Muslim Turkic and Mongol peoples, referred to as Tartars. The exterior of the Tartar Tent consisted of metal sheeting painted to resemble the folds of a nomad's tent. The walls inside were decorated with Toile de Jouy. Although the original structure disappeared, a modern replica was donated to the Désert de Retz by the Ugine A.C.G. steel company in 1989.[149]

Another tribute to Islam in a picturesque garden is found in the Steinfurter Bagno near Burgsteinfurt, Westphalia, built from 1765 to 1787. In addition to a pyramid with a thatched roof, the garden boasts a Chinese Palace remarkably similar to Monville's Chinese House, and a mosque with two minarets. Cahiers XVIII and XIX of Georges Le Rouge, with colored plates, are devoted to this garden.

---

[149] The structure utilized steel sheets plated with a tin-lead alloy, known as terne, traditionally used to coat steel to prevent corrosion.

One of the artists who collaborated with Georges-Louis Le Rouge in his herculean project was Francesco Bettini (c. 1737-1815), a gifted and multi-talented Italian who—like Monville—was largely ignored until the mid-1990's. Bettini spent 1772-1774 and 1778-1784 in France, immersing himself in landscape design and visiting numerous gardens. He accompanied Le Rouge to some of the gardens and visited others on his own, making numerous sketches for Le Rouge, who noted, "*On peut dire que Bettini est réellement plein de genie.*" Le Rouge considered Bettini to be a "genius." Half the images in Cahier XI and a third of those in Cahier XII—both published in 1784—are by Bettini. Although Bettini visited and made drawings of the Désert de Retz, Le Rouge did not incorporate them in Cahier XIII; he also declined to publish Bettini's drawings of many other gardens including the Parc Monceau, Moulin Joli, Romainville, Choisy, Bellevue, Pontchartrain and Bonnelles. Bettini's drawings of the Désert de Retz are recorded in the second of his two albums entitled *Caos e Farraggine*, preserved in the Archivo Doria-Pamphilij in Rome; some of them were published in the late 1970's and 1980's. In his authoritative essay on Bettini, [150] David L. Hays reproduced a "remarkable" sketch by Bettini, also in the second album, of a visibly pregnant Marie Antoinette crossing a stone footbridge in the garden

---

[150] "Francesco Bettini and the Pedagogy of Garden Design," in *Tradition and Innovation in French Garden Art: Chapters of a New History*, edited by John Dixon Hunt and Michael Conan, University of Pennsylvania Press, 2002.

of the Petit Trianon in the company of her head gardener Antoine Richard, walking behind her and sheltering her with a parasol. Bettini also depicted himself standing to the right, sketching the scene. He noted that the queen was making arrangements for a *fête de nuit* in honor of her brother, Joseph II, the Holy Roman Emperor, an event that took place on August 4, 1781.

Francesco Bettini was not only a talented landscape artist, but an accomplished musician, performing on both violin and viola at the salon hosted by Madame de Tessé in her townhouse on the Rue de Varenne and her château in Chaville. Both Thomas Jefferson and Gouverneur Morris were her guests; after visiting Chaville, Jefferson undertook an extensive correspondence with her that ended only with her death.

In addition to the views of the Désert de Retz published by Le Rouge, a number of maps and illustrations of the garden were produced in the late 18th and early 19th centuries.

On November 24, 2006, a colored drawing by Louis Enslen[151] entitled *Points de vue d'un Jardin anglais appellé le Désert sictué dans la Forêt de Marli* was auctioned in Budapest. This document, probably executed in the mid-1780's, measures 64.5 high by 96.5 centimeters wide (25.4" by 38") and consists of seven panels. A large horizontal illustration in the

---

[151] Also written "Ensslin."

center entitled "Plan Général du Jardin" depicts an aerial view of the Désert de Retz, and is flanked on each side by three smaller panels. Beneath the central picture is an "Explication," with the titles of each of the small panels:

1. Vue de la Terrasse
2. Projet à Exécuter
3. Vue du Pavillon Chinois
4. Vue du Pont Gotique [sic]
5. Vue du Temple
6. Vue de la Colonne Cannelée

These illustrations are interesting for numerous reasons. First of all, the "Terrasse" is actually the Open-air Theater, with its stands of elm trees on either side. The "Projet à Exécuter" appears to be an aqueduct, envisaged but never built. The fourth panel depicts the Temple of Repose, but the "Gothic Bridge" may have been one of the ephemeral structures that Monville commissioned for his garden. The "Vue du Temple," showing not only the Temple of Pan but the Chinese House, is similar to the work by Constant Bourgeois reproduced in this book. Monville's Column House, rendered in the sixth panel, is swathed in greenery, confirming written descriptions.

Even though photography would not be invented until the nineteenth century, there were numerous opportunities for Frenchmen as wealthy as Monville to commission portraits or sculpted busts. An

Englishwoman who visited the Grand Hôtel de Monville in 1777 mentions having seen such a portrait.

In a popular Paris studio, customers sat for true-to-life portraits created by a device known as the physionotrace, invented by a court cellist named Gilles-Louis Chrétien (1754-1811) who, with his business partner Edmé Quenedey des Ricets (1756-1839), opened their studio at 45, Rue des Bons-Enfants, near the Palais Royal, on June 26, 1788. American emissaries Thomas Jefferson and Gouverneur Morris sat for their portraits on the same day, April 23, 1789. [152] By November of 1789, Chrétien and Quenedey had produced over a thousand portraits. Monville, too, was probably a customer, since he frequented the Palais Royal neighborhood on a daily basis while in Paris; yet nothing has turned up.

Monville's circle of acquaintances included many painters and sculptors. Portrait sculptors such as Jean-Antoine Houdon (1741-1828) or Augustin Pajou (1730-1809) could certainly have produced sculptures for Monville.

Madame Vigée Le Brun recounted her meeting with Monsieur de Monville in 1786 at Madame du Barry's château in nearby Louveciennes. She found

---

[152] Illustrations of the physionotrace and the portraits of Jefferson and Morris are reproduced in *Thomas Jefferson's Paris*, by Professor Howard C. Rice, Jr., published by the Princeton University Press in 1991.

Monville *"aimable et très élégant,"* and expressed so much interest in his Désert that Monville escorted her there personally for a guided tour.

Madame Vigée Le Brun was not only renowned for her painting but, like Sophie Arnould, was a *salonnière* and counted Monville among her guests. Some have suggested that she painted Monville's portrait; if so, its whereabouts are currently unknown. A drawing in red pencil and stump by Louis Roland Trinquesse (1746-1800) entitled, *Man Playing the Guitar, Seated in an Armchair*, in the collection of the interior designer Elsie de Wolfe, Lady Mendl (1865? - 1950),[153] was sold at auction on December 9, 1981. Based on several written descriptions, there is an intriguing possibility that this drawing could be a representation of Monsieur de Monville.[154] Additionally, although there is written evidence that Monville was an accomplished harpist and flautist, Dufort de Cheverny wrote that Monville, like many of his contemporaries, was *"assez musicien pour toucher de tous les instruments;"* [155] consequently, playing the guitar would not be considered beyond his capacities.

Carmontelle executed portraits of scores of French

---

[153] Diana Ketcham reports that Lady Mendl had visited the Désert de Retz when it was still closed to the public.

[154] This drawing is reproduced in monochrome in the catalogue of the auction, conducted by Ader-Nordmann.

[155] "Such an accomplished musician that he was able to play any instrument."

154

aristocrats and commoners as well as English visitors such as Laurence Sterne, author of *Tristram Shandy*; the philosopher David Hume and the Shakespearian actor David Garrick.

Around 1762, Carmontelle depicted Monville's niece, Thomasse-Thérèse, in a collective portrait entitled *La duchesse de Gramont, Madame de Stainville et le comte de Biron,* now housed in the collection of the Musée Condé in Chantilly. François-Anatole Gruyer[156] reports that Thomasse-Thérèse appeared to be something of a hell-raiser as a young wife: after an "adventure" with an actor named Clairval[157] and other behavior considered scandalous, her husband, exasperated, dispatched his wayward spouse to a convent in Nancy, where she "changed her ways and became a model of Christian humility" and remained until her death in 1789.[158]

As mentioned previously, Thomasse-Thérèse had given birth to two daughters, Marie Stéphanie de Choiseul-Stainvilleand Françoise-Thérèse, the unfortunate Princess of Monaco who died on the guillotine. Of the other two subjects who sat for the portrait, Thomasse-Therese's sister-in-law, Béatrix de Choiseul-Stainville, duchesse de Gramont (born in 1730), was a bibliophile and salonist; she died on

---

[156] Gruyer, François-Anatole, *Les Portraits de Carmontelle: Chantilly,* Chantilly, Éditeur Scientifique, 1902.

[157] Born Jean-Baptiste Guignard on April 27, 1735, he died in obscurity in 1795.

[158] According to Professor Bongie, wives engaging in "infidelities and conjugal misadventures" were often forcefully confined to nunneries.

the guillotine on April 17, 1794 (28 Germinal II). Armand-Louis de Gontaut Biron (born in 1747) was one of the French generals who fought for American independence, notably at Yorktown. He, too, was executed on the guillotine, on December 31, 1793 (11 Nivôse II). Thomasse-Thérèse herself died in 1789 at the age of forty-three.

Cendres and Radiguet suggest that Carmontelle may have also painted a portrait of Monville. The author of this book has identified five portraits of unidentified male subjects by Carmontelle auctioned in recent years, any of which could have been Monville. Portraits or sketches of Monsieur de Monville are also believed to have been executed by other artists. If any portraits do exist, however, their whereabouts are unknown to the general public. Some have suggested that the living descendants of Monsieur de Monville's only sibling, his elder sister Marie-Henriette, may possess a portrait of their distant relative. Documents relating to Monville and his sister's descendants may also exist in the Monegasque archives.

On May 7, 1784, Congress appointed Thomas Jefferson as minister plenipotentiary to join John Adams and Benjamin Franklin in negotiating treaties of amity and commerce with European nations.

On July 5, 1784, Jefferson sailed for Europe from Boston, accompanied by his 12-year-old daughter Martha (Patsy), William Short (1759-1849), a young relative and protégé who had trained as a lawyer and was engaged by Jefferson as his private secretary, and by Jefferson's manservant James Hemings, a 19-year-old mixed-race slave, who was promptly apprenticed to a Paris caterer, since Jefferson wanted him to learn "the art of cookery."[159]

Jefferson and his party arrived in Le Havre on August 3, 1784, and continued on to Paris. They first resided in the Hôtel de Landron and then at the Hôtel de Langeac on the Champs-Elysées,[160] built on the plans of Jean-François-Thérèse Chalgrin (1739-1811), the architect who designed the Arc de Triomphe in Paris.

At about the same time, Abigail Adams, accompanied by her children John Quincy and Abigail (Nabby) arrived in Paris to join her husband, who would be subsequently appointed the first ambassador to the Court of St. James's in London. John and Abigail Adams disliked Paris, so they rented a large house in the suburban village of Auteuil that had previously belonged to two sisters, Marie and Geneviève Rainteau de Verrières, both retired actresses, and lived there from August 1784 to May 1785. The Hôtel des Demoiselles de Verrières still stands; previously the corporate headquarters of the energy conglomerate Total, it is

---

[159] Jefferson's other daughter, nine-year old Mary (Polly), accompanied by the 14-year old slave Sally Hemings, did not arrive in France until three years later, in July 1787.

[160] The building, located at 92, Avenue des Champs-Elysées, no longer exists.

now occupied by a French scientific organization.

The puritanical Adamses are generally considered to have disliked the French, but historian David McCullough suggests that John Adams held French women in high regard. He wrote to Abigail, "I admire the ladies here. They are handsome, and very well educated. Their accomplishments are exceedingly brilliant. And their knowledge of letters and arts exceeds that of the English ladies."[161] And, "The longer I live in Europe and the longer I consider our affairs, the more important our alliance with France appears to me." Abigail Adams later wrote, "Nobody ever leaves Paris but with a degree of tristeness."

It is possible that John and Abigail Adams might have attended a dinner party at the Grand Hôtel de Monville or been escorted to the Désert de Retz by the Count de Chaumont or another of their French acquaintances.

In the summer of 1786, Jefferson was introduced to Maria Cosway by the American artist John Trumbull, a portraitist and historical painter, whose *Declaration of Independence* (1817) is reproduced on the reverse of the two-dollar bill. Cosway was a talented Italian-born English artist who, according to Diana Ketcham, "made a marriage of convenience to a wealthy and eccentric London society painter, Richard Cosway." She and Jefferson, a widower,

---

[161] McCullough, David, *John Adams*, Simon & Schuster, 2002.

developed a close personal relationship; it is most probable that Jefferson fell in love with her.

Marie Goebel Kimball writes breathlessly:

> On the sixteenth of September 1786, Jefferson and Mrs. Cosway set out on an excursion neither of them was ever to forget.[162] It was to the Désert de Retz a garden in the Anglo-Chinese style situated about four miles from Saint-Germain-en-Laye. Here, indeed, was brought to life everything Jefferson had dreamed of for his own garden, and more than his fancy ever beheld...Small wonder Jefferson exclaimed, in recalling the scene to Mrs. Cosway, "How grand the idea excited by the remains of such a column!"

It is possible that Jefferson learned about the Désert de Retz from his secretary William Short who, at Jefferson's recommendation, had spent the winter of 1784-85 as a paying guest of the Royer family in Saint-Germain-en-Laye in order to improve his French. [163] Chambourcy is adjacent to Saint-Germain, so Short may have undertaken an excursion to the Désert and reported his discovery.

Jefferson was particularly impressed by the ground floor plan of Monville's Column House, where oval rooms filled out a circular space. Cendres and Radiguet speculate that Jefferson may have visited

---

[162] A reënactment of this event was shot on location at the Désert de Retz in 1994 by James Ivory for his film, *Jefferson in Paris*.

[163] Short, age 26, promptly fell in love with the Royers' 16-year old daughter, Anne-Hypolyte-Louise, nicknamed Lilite, whom he consecrated "La Belle de Saint-Germain."

the Désert de Retz on more than one occasion and even sojourned there as Monville's guest.

The Cosways left Paris on October 5, 1786. On October 12, 1786, after recovering from a dislocated wrist, Thomas Jefferson wrote Maria Cosway his *Dialogue between My Head and My Heart*, in which the two debate the conflicting merits of love and pleasure on the one hand, and intellect and rationality on the other. In the letter to Cosway, Jefferson evokes their visit to the Désert.[164]

Like Monsieur de Monville, Maria Cosway was an accomplished harpist, performing her compositions at musical evenings in her London townhouse. Although Jefferson may have been infatuated with Maria Cosway, based on her correspondence, Kimball judges her to have been "a spoiled, egocentric young woman, with a very limited emotional capacity." Regardless of her putative character flaws, Cosway and Jefferson continued to correspond until his death in 1826.

Jefferson and Maria Cosway also visited the Château de Bagatelle in the Bois de Boulogne, designed by François-Joseph Bélanger and built in 1777, five years before Monville's Column House.[165] The ground floors of both buildings bear a

---

[164] Jefferson and John Adams had visited the Stowe Landscape Gardens together in April 1786 in what Abigail Adams described as their "journey into the country."

[165] See Baillio, Joseph, "Hubert Robert's Decorations for the Château of Bagatelle," in *Metropolitan Museum Journal 27*, 1992.

certain resemblance. Jefferson proposed curvilinear floor plans with oval rooms for the renovations at the Hôtel de Langeac, his design for the Capitol building in Washington—which was not accepted—and the Rotunda at the University of Virginia in Charlottesville—which was.

It is also possible that the skylight in Monsieur de Monville's Column House influenced Jefferson when he designed the plans for Poplar Forest, his retreat located in Bedford County, VA, the first octagonal house built in America. Jefferson especially liked the light-filled interiors in France, and both the skylight in the dining room and the floor-to-ceiling windows in the parlor at Poplar Forest are French touches.

In June 1789, Thomas Jefferson, meeting with the Marquis de Lafayette, drafted a charter of rights that became the basis for the *Declaration of the Rights of Man and the Citizen* that Lafayette presented to the National Assembly the following month. Jefferson again met secretly with Lafayette and other French liberals to discuss a new French Constitution in August 1789.

On September 26, 1789, the American Senate confirmed Jefferson as Secretary of State. Two days later he sailed to America from Le Havre, unaware of his appointment until he arrived at Norfolk, VA, on November 23.

Jefferson was succeeded in Paris by his protégé William Short, who served as chargé d'affaires from 1790 to 1792. In addition to dispatching Jefferson eye-witness accounts of the unfolding French Revolution, Short was the hero of what Marie Goebel Kimball termed with her usual hyperbole "the most roman romantic love affair in which an American had ever been engaged" by falling under the charm of a member of one of the noblest families in France, Alexandrine Charlotte Sophie de Rohan-Chabot (1763-1839).

Rosalie de la Rochefoucauld, as she was known, had been married to an uncle 20 years her senior, Louis-Alexandre de la Rochefoucauld (1743-1792), a friend of Franklin, Jefferson and Lafayette. The fact that Rosalie was married did not deter Short's ardor, and he pursued her assiduously. His sentiments appear to have been reciprocated; the couple exchanged hundreds of love letters, some of which Kimball published in 1926.[166]

Rosalie's husband was stoned to death before her eyes in 1792, the same year in which Short was confirmed as minister resident to the Netherlands. Short soon departed from France, leaving his Rosalie who, in a sense, became a double widow. But she did not wear widow's weeds for long, for in 1810 she married General Boniface Louis de Castellane (1758-1837).

---

[166] Kimball, Marie Goebel, "William Short, Jefferson's Only 'Son,'" in *The North American Review*, September, 1926.

Short was succeeded by Gouverneur Morris,[167] who had arrived in Paris in 1789 to conduct business and who served from 1792 to 1794, the only foreign envoy to remain in France during the Reign of Terror. Two months after he was briefly arrested in March of 1793 despite his diplomatic immunity, Morris moved to a country house he rented in the town of Seine-Port (previously known as Saint-Port), three and a half hours ride from Paris, only returning briefly to Paris until he left France in October 1794. Although one of the American Founding Fathers and the author of parts of the Constitution including the Preamble, and although he advocated religious tolerance and opposed slavery, Morris was nevertheless a patrician, critical of the French Revolution, frequenting and aiding counter-revolutionaries and supporting the deposed monarch, Louis XVI, and Marie Antoinette, whom he attempted unsuccessfully to save from execution as much out of compassion as from his political beliefs. Morris maintained that a monarchy was the form of government best suited for France because, as Stephen O'Shea wrote in an article published in 1998, Morris believed that "few Frenchmen were capable of managing the affairs of their country in a democratic manner."[168] Despite or, perhaps, because

---

[167] "Gouverneur" was his mother's maiden name. She was the descendant of French Protestants who first fled to Holland, thence to New Amsterdam (New York) in 1663.

[168] "Shrewd Liaisons: The devilish diplomacy of Gouverneur Morris during the French Revolution," published in *Elle* (US) in 1998 and on stephenosheaonline.com.

of a wooden leg—according to O'Shea, Morris's left leg had been amputated after he was reportedly run over by a phaeton as he was escaping an irate husband who had caught him *in flagrante delicto* with the latter's wife—Morris was a seductive libertine who engaged in a longstanding affair in both Paris and Hamburg with Madame de Flahaut, née Adélaïde-Marie-Émilie Filleul (1761-1836), previously the mistress of Talleyrand and the mother of his son, known as Charles de Flahaut (1785-1870). Morris sedulously documented their trysts, sometimes in graphic detail, in the entries in his diary. He was so proficient in French that he could compose rhymed verses to accompany bouquets of flowers he sent her, and Adélaïde was fluent in English. Born in 1726, Adélaïde's husband Charles-François de Flahaut de la Billarderie was 36 years her senior; he died on the guillotine in 1794.

Both lovers were eventually married, but not to each other. In 1802, Adélaïde wed Portuguese diplomat José Maria de Souza-Botelho (1758-1825), whom she had met in Hamburg. After escorting the wife and children of his friend and business partner James Le Ray across the Atlantic in 1798, Morris, a lifelong bachelor, married Anne Cary Randolph, a cousin of Martha Jefferson, in 1809, when he was 57 years old.

Not only did Morris dislike John Paul Jones, the naval hero who had been knighted by King Louis XVI, he despised another British-born American patriot, Thomas Paine, whom he considered "no more than a drunk." Paine had emigrated to America in 1774, where he wrote *Common Sense*, advocating independence, published in 1776. He returned to Europe and, in March 1791, wrote *The Rights of Man*, which sold hundreds of thousands of copies and made Paine so popular in revolutionary France that he was granted honorary French citizenship by the Legislative Assembly on October 10, 1792, along with Washington, Hamilton and Madison. Paine was then elected to the French National Convention from the *département* of Pas de Calais, although he was unable to speak French. When the Convention was in session, he would sit beside one of his English-speaking colleagues such as Georges Danton, Nicolas de Condorcet or Jacques-Pierre Brissot, who would interpret the debates and whisper the translations to him.

Daniel Jouve reports in his book, *Paris: Birthplace of the U.S.A,* that, "Paine had many ideas that were ahead of his time: free education for all children, retirement at sixty, the right of workers to negotiate salaries and working conditions, relief for the aged and sick, a progressive income tax, the abolition of slavery and equality of the sexes." In 1791!

Unfortunately, Paine voted against the death penalty for Louis XVI, proposing instead that the king be exiled to America, "where he could learn the meaning of democracy." Despite his American nationality, Paine was arrested on December 28,

1793, and awaited execution in the building that today houses the French Senate—the Luxembourg Palace—where he began writing a deist tract destined to become a bestseller in America. Paine's *The Age of Reason* challenges institutionalized religion and the legitimacy of the Bible and rejects revelation and authority as a source of religious knowledge.

Paine languished long after most detainees—such as Monville—had been freed. The reason: Gouverneur Morris declined to demand the release of this unjustifiably incarcerated American citizen. Paine's situation was complicated because the French insisted that he had acquired French nationality. Morris did intervene with the French to free other imprisoned Americans, including William Hoskins, arrested upon landing at Calais; Thomas Waters Griffith, in France to sell American tobacco; and William Jackson, seeking buyers for American lands owned by his wealthy brother-in-law, the future senator William Bingham. It was not until Morris was replaced by James Monroe[169] that Paine was freed on November 5, 1794. Monroe then invited Paine to reside as his guest in his private residence. Thomas Paine remained in France until 1802, returning to the United States at President Jefferson's invitation. He died in New York on June 8, 1809.

---

[169] Four future presidents of the United States lived in Paris during Monville's lifetime: Thomas Jefferson, John Adams, John Quincy Adams and James Monroe.

Although it will probably never be known as a certainty, given Thomas Paine's circle of French notables and the high esteem in which he was held in France, and given Monsieur de Monville's sympathy for the American cause, it is not inconceivable that Paine, too, may have known Monsieur de Monville and been his guest.

After the Désert de Retz

"The Chinese Pavilion in the Park of the Desert," by Constant Bourgeois (1767-1841), engraved by De Saulx and reproduced in *Le Nouveau Jardin Français* by Alexandre de Laborde, published in 1808.

En traversant la Révolution, Monville trouva cependant le secret de mourir dans son lit et d'obtenir la grâce des Sylla et des Marius français qui n'en faisaient à personne.
--Alexandre de Tilly

François Racine de Monville, who had a wide circle of acquaintances, not only among nobility at the court in Versailles, but among poets, musicians, artists, philosophers and sportsmen, realized that the political ferment and dissatisfaction with the status quo in France were reaching the boiling point. That point was reached on July 14, 1789, with the storming and subsequent dismantling of the Bastille, a medieval fortress in eastern Paris.

Knowing of his status as the grandson of one of the hated tax farmers, and aware that his companionship with the nobility represented a potential danger, Monville read the handwriting on the wall and, with a foreboding of what was to come, decided to dispose of his real estate holdings both in Paris and Chambourcy.

In 1790, Monville offered his two Paris residences to his longstanding friend, Pierre-Augustin Caron de Beaumarchais, for 400,000 *livres*. Despite the fact that Beaumarchais was now wealthy from his ownership of a company that supplied drinking water to Parisians, he declined the offer, replying that "the price was too high and the interior too gaudy." Instead, he engaged the services of a young architect, Paul Guillaume Lemoine le Romain (1755-?), who designed a lavish residence across from where the Bastille once stood. Hubert Robert was commissioned to decorate the Grand Salon with landscapes ornamented with antique statuary,[170] and François-Joseph Bélanger laid out a picturesque garden. Beaumarchais died in 1799, after a long and adventurous life, and was laid to rest in the Père Lachaise Cemetery in Paris.

Finally, on July 20 and 21, 1792, Monsieur de Monville succeeded in liquidating his Paris residences and the Désert de Retz through a sale to a singular English Francophile, Lewis Disney-Ffytche[171] (1738-1822) of Swinderby, Lincolnshire, who had married the daughter of the governor of Bengal. The price of the Désert was 108,000 *livres*, and the Grand and Petit Hôtels de Monville were sold for 275,000 *livres*—all of it in "convertible currency." The transactions were conducted by *Maître* Pierre Tiron, a *notaire* who handled some of Monville's legal affairs.[172]

It is worth noting that, before purchasing Monville's properties, Disney-Ffytche had acquired in February 1782 another large townhouse, the Hôtel de Boynes, as well as a group of houses erected in 1555 on the corner of the Rue Pavée and the Rue des Francs-Bourgeois, known as the Basse-cour Lamoignon. It

---

[170] Although the building itself was demolished in 1818, parts of these paintings were transferred to the Paris Town Hall.

[171] Born Lewis Disney, he added his wife's maiden name to his upon their marriage. Ffytche is one of several proper names commencing with the initial *ff* digraph. Others are Fforde and ffrench.

[172] A *notaire* is a lawyer specializing in contracts, succession planning and real estate transactions. They are addressed by the honorific, *Maître*.

would seem that the Englishman was speculating in real estate as so many other wealthy individuals were at the time: his sojourn in France allowed him to combine business with pleasure.

All of Lewis Disney-Ffytche's holdings in Paris and Chambourcy were seized by the Revolutionary authorities in 1793 [173] but, after prolonged legal wrangling, he succeeded in recouping all his sequestered properties.

According to Pierre Robin, writing in *Le Séquestre des biens ennemis sous la Révolution française,* Disney-Ffytche sold the Grand Hôtel de Monville for 149,500 francs on March 12, 1808, to the statesman and diplomat Charles-Maurice de Talleyrand-Périgord (1754-1838).

To escape the Reign of Terror, Talleyrand had lived in exile in the United States from 1794 to 1796. The houseguest of then-Senator Aaron Burr (1756-1836), he worked in a bank and speculated in commodities and real estate. After being tried for treason—and acquitted—in 1807, Burr emigrated to Europe, but Talleyrand declined to reciprocate Burr's hospitality since Talleyrand had been friends with Alexander Hamilton, whom Burr had killed in a duel. Hamilton was born in 1775 on Nevis, in the Leeward Islands, the illegitimate son of a Scot, James Hamilton, and a French Huguenot, Rachel

---

[173] The Paris properties were sequestered on 11 Brumaire and the Désert de Retz on 29 Brumaire II, corresponding to November 1 and 19, 1793.

Faucette Lavien. After relocating first to Saint-Croix, then to New York at the age of seventeen, he become one of the Founding Fathers and the first United States Secretary of the Treasury.

Talleyrand's chef was the renowned Marie-Antonin Carême (1784-1833), whose edible architecture—multi-layered cakes in the shapes of ruins and bizarre-shaped buildings, including those of the Désert de Retz—were the origin of his nickname, the Palladio of Pastry.

The Duc de Dalberg (1777-1833) acquired the Grand Hôtel de Monville in 1811, and Talleyrand bought the Hôtel de Saint-Florentin on the Place de la Concorde, built in 1769 from the plans of Chalgrin. The U.S. State Department purchased the building from the Rothschild Family in 1950.

Before leaving the Grand Hôtel de Monville, Talleyrand's estranged wife, Catherine Noele Grand de Talleyrand, (1762-1834)[174] dismantled one of the rooms of the Grand Hôtel de Monville and partially reconstructed Monville's decorative wood paneling in the house she had acquired, the Hôtel de Cassini, located at 32, Rue de Babylone, in the Seventh Arrondissement of Paris, where it remains today. The building is currently occupied by a French government agency and is not open to the public.

---

[174] Catherine Grand, née Worlée, was born in the Danish possession of Trankebar in India and, at age 16, had married George Francis Grand, a British civil servant of Huguenot origin.

Pierre Robin reports that the Petit Hôtel de Monville was acquired in 1824 by Louis XVI's former minister of war, the Marquis Frédéric-Séraphin de La Tour du Pin (1759-1837) [175] and then, in 1835, by the Italian patriot and woman of letters, Princess Christine de Belgiojoso (1808-1871).

There can be no doubt that Monville, ably advised by his Swiss banker, Jean-Frédéric Perregaux, succeeded in protecting the proceeds of the sale of his property, and that these funds were the source of his income for the rest of his life: his death notice gives his profession as *rentier*—that is, an annuitant.

Perregaux, who was born in Neuchâtel in 1744, was another of the more complex and enthralling of Monville's acquaintances, possibly introduced to him by one of their mutual acquaintances such as Bertrand Barère de Vieuzac or Beaumarchais, both of whom were Perregaux's clients. Arriving in Paris in 1765, Perregaux first worked for his compatriot Jacques Necker before establishing his own bank in 1781. Perregaux shared Monville's fondness for the theater, the opera and beautiful women: he was known as *le plus mondain des banquiers*. Like Monville, Perregaux subscribed to a season ticket for a reserved seat at the Opera.

Perregaux was gifted with the ability to befriend players from many sides at the same time; his clients

---

[175] The Marquis de la Tour de Pin accompanied Lafayette's forces fighting for American independence and was a member of the Society of the Cincinnati

included not only the British ambassador and other diplomats, but numerous other English aristocrats such as Disney-Ffytche and British spies, among them the infamous Nathaniel Parker-Forth (1744-1809), who obtained and sold in London Madame du Barry's jewelry collection purloined during the night of January 10-11, 1791. Notable among Perregaux's large feminine clientele were Grace Dalrymple Elliott and Catherine Noele Grand de Talleyrand, who lodged with Perregaux's in-laws upon her arrival in Paris from Calcutta.

Perregaux was also Gouverneur Morris's landlord in the early 1790's when Morris was serving as the American emissary to France, and is known to have invited him to dinner. It is possible that Monville met Morris through Perregaux; lively conversation would have been easy whether or not Monville spoke English, since Morris was fluent in French.

Perregaux also acted as a discrete intermediary between certain British diplomats and American representatives, including Thomas Jefferson. He rapidly attached himself to the revolutionary movements in France and, through these associations, was able to speculate on commodities for his clients in Switzerland and London. He also worked for the French Convention and Robespierre's *Comité du Salut Public*, for which he obtained funds through his contacts in Switzerland. Although briefly jailed in September 1793, he was shortly released thanks to the efforts of Bertrand

Barère de Vieuzac. After the death of his wife in January 1794, events compelled Perregaux to briefly seek refuge in his homeland.

A skilled and cunning survivor and a political chameleon, Perregaux ended his career as the regent of the Bank of France under Napoleon Bonaparte. Perregaux died in 1808 and his remains were enshrined in the Pantheon in Paris, the only Swiss so honored.

The Goncourt brothers painted a flattering portrait of Perregaux in their *Histoire de la société française sous le Directoire*, cited by Ernest Boysse. Rarely has a banker has been described with such effusive praise:

> In those times of financial troubles, was [Perregaux] not the confessor of needs, the providence of artists? He guided them in their investments, he gave them his time, he opened his purse...He was a patron of the arts, a benefactor a generous protector, who appeared to lend money against his will. This man of money was more attuned to the art world than to that of finance... From before the French Revolution through the Directorate he continued to be a good friend and a wise counselor...the banker to those who had wealth, the salvation of those who had nothing and a trustee to everyone.

Among Perregaux's numerous feminine clients was Marie-Madeleine Guimard (1743-1816), one of the most highly acclaimed *danseuses* of her day. In 1773, she commissioned Claude-Nicolas Ledoux to design a luxurious neo-classical *hôtel particulier* known as the Temple of Terpsichore, located on the Rue de la Chaussée d'Antin in Paris, and engaged the painter Jean-Honoré Fragonard (1732-1806) to decorate the interiors.

La Guimard hosted a lavish reception on May 4, 1778, to celebrate the wedding of her fifteen-year old daughter, also named Marie-Madeleine, whose father, Jean-Benjamin de La Borde (1734-1794), one of Monville's youthful companions, was a tax farmer and composer. Diana Ketcham reports that Monsieur de Monville, who "had agreed to stand up for the groom," a goldsmith named Robert Arnould Claude Drais (c.1750-?), was in attendance at the reception. "Unfortunate marriage," according to Edmond de Goncourt in his biography of La Guimard, "That ended after a year with the death of the young bride."

An anecdote cited in a profile of Perregaux by "Jean-Bernard," nom de plume of Jean-Bernard Passerieu (1858-1936), in the December 9, 1928, issue of *Dimanche Illustré*, perfectly illustrates Perregaux's munificence towards his clients combined with a steely self-interest.

Jean-Bernard relates that, when La Guimard was invited to perform in London, she entrusted her savings to Perregaux but, since she spent lavishly, her account was quickly depleted and she was compelled to dispose of her townhouse. To maximize the profit from the sale, she offered it as the prize in a raffle, selling the tickets for 100 *livres* apiece. Naturally, Perregaux drew the winning ticket—one can only imagine how much he spent purchasing as many tickets as possible—and he transferred the headquarters of his bank to the building that "had witnessed so many brilliant festivities and so many frivolous soirées."[176]

With a banker as solicitous as Perregaux minding the financial affairs of his "artist" friend, there can be little doubt that Monville was in good hands. What we may find significant is that in 1792—the same year that Monville sold all his properties—Perregaux transferred enormous sums of money to Switzerland, the destination of his frequent voyages.

It is also important to consider the potential effects on Monville's fortunes of the hyperinflation that France underwent between 1789 and 1797 as the result of the introduction of a type of fiat paper money known as *assignats*.

In the spring of 1789, with the government bankrupt, the National Assembly decreed the issuance of a total of 400 million *livres* worth of interest-bearing *assignat*s, secured by the properties confiscated from the crown and the Catholic Church.

During the debates in the National Assembly, the proponents of the paper money were led by Jean-

[176] Jean-Bernard, "Le Banquier Perregaux," *Dimanche Illustré*, le 9 décembre 1920.

Paul Marat and Honoré Mirabeau; their main adversaries were Jacques Necker and the physiocrat Pierre Samuel du Pont de Nemours, who opposed the measures on economic grounds, arguing that the new currency would be followed by additional emissions with their consequent depreciation. They predicted that the calamities of the Scots economist John Law's Mississippi Bubble [177] would be re-enacted across republican France.

The objections and warnings of Jacques Necker and Du Pont de Nemours were ridiculed and brushed aside. The brilliant orators who defended the printing of *assignats* ignored the lessons of recent history and convinced themselves that "This time it's different," a phrase reiterated by many others before and after to their everlasting sorrow.

Among their specious arguments, the enthusiasts claimed that the laws of economics did not apply to France, that the lesson of John Law's failed experiment was not to issue excessive quantities of paper money, that a republican government could more safely inflate its currency than a monarchy and that the *assignats* were backed by the immense landed wealth of France.

---

[177] The Mississippi Bubble was a financial scheme that triggered a speculative frenzy in France from 1717 to 1720 and ended in financial collapse. The scheme was engineered by a Scots economist, John Law, (1671-1729), who had emigrated to France after being condemned to death for killing a rival in a duel.

The French parliamentarians did not only have the prophetic example of the collapse of Law's system: the American colonists had issued Continental currency as early as 1775. The banknotes, designed by Benjamin Franklin, were not only aesthetically pleasing, but incorporated ingenious security features to foil counterfeiters.[178] Between the years of 1775 and 1781, a staggering total of $241,552,780 in Continental currency was issued to finance the war effort. The fate of this fiat paper money can be summed up concisely in the phrase, "Not worth a Continental."

Ignoring the historical precedents, in the autumn of 1789 the French National Assembly approved the issuance of an additional 800 million *livres* of noninterest-bearing notes and decreed that a total of no more than 1.2 billion *livres* could be issued. Despite this stated limit, nine months later another 600 million *livres* were approved.

Realizing that his defense of sound money was falling on deaf ears, Necker resigned in 1790 and, after his wife's death in 1794, returned to his native Switzerland, where he died in 1804. Du Pont de Nemours was condemned to death because of his support for Louis XVI and Marie Antoinette but,

---

[178] The obverse was printed in two colors, and the reverse of each denomination bore a "nature print," an intricate engraving of the leaves of a different plant. To create them, Franklin placed a leaf on a damp cloth, which was then pressed on a bed of soft plaster. When hardened, the plaster had a negative impression of the leaf. Molten copper was then poured over the plaster to cast the printing plate.

like Monville, was spared from the guillotine due to the fall of Robespierre and relocated with his two sons and their families to Rhode Island. He became a friend of Jefferson and was instrumental in the purchase of the Louisiana Territory in 1803.

In September 1791, *assignat*s totaling 300 million *livres* were issued. In April of 1792 another 300 million was approved. Prices rose, but wages didn't keep up and in 1793 a mob plundered 200 stores in Paris. Price controls were imposed by the Law of the Maximum but, since farmers and manufacturers found themselves selling at a loss, output decreased and much of what was produced was hoarded. Rationing was then implemented. To compel acceptance of its paper money, the government imposed a 20-year prison sentence on anyone selling the *assignat*s at a discount and dictated a death sentence for anyone differentiating between paper *livres* and gold or silver specie in setting prices.

To make matters worse, because they lacked Franklin's sophisticated security features, the *assignats* were easy to counterfeit: millions of phony *assignats* were printed, especially in England, and circulated in France, where they contributed to popular distrust of paper money and accelerated the hyperinflation.

By 1794, 7 billion *livres* in *assignat*s were in circulation. In May 1795 this total reached 10 billion *livres,* and by July 1795 it had risen to 14 billion *livres*. When the total reached 45 billion *livres,* the printing plates for the *assignat*s were publically smashed in the Place Vendôme in Paris. A new type of paper money, called a *mandat*, was issued, but within two years the *mandats* lost 97 percent of their value. The printing plates for *mandats* were also publically destroyed.

Naturally, the wealthy were able to profit enormously during the period by speculation: purchasing hard assets such as real estate with increasingly worthless paper money. When it was all over, only the poor and the landless were left holding the bag, filled to the brim with worthless scraps of paper. The perceptive Gouverneur Morris had foretold the demise of the *assignats*—and of fiat money in general—when he wrote to William Short on April 7, 1790, "Paper thou art and unto Paper thou shalt return."

Finally, in 1803, under Napoleon Bonaparte, a 20-franc gold piece was introduced, and a bimetallic monetary system based on gold and silver remained in effect in France until 1914.

We know that Monville sold his properties in 1792, at the height of the *assignat* hyperinflation. We also know that the purchaser, Disney-Ffytche, was English and that Monville's banker, Perregaux, was Swiss. Considering these facts, we may surmise that Monville was successful in safeguarding a substantial portion of his net worth outside of France, thereby protecting himself from the depreciation of the currency that resulted in the ruin of so many others.

After the sale of his properties, Monville moved into rented quarters in the Rue Neuve des Mathurins in Paris with his companion Sarah, a young actress in the company of Marguerite Brunet (1739-1820), a thespian and theater director known by the sobriquet Mademoiselle Montansier.

Mademoiselle Montansier led a highly adventurous life and was involved romantically with numerous men. Born in Bayonne, she fled from the Ursuline convent in Bordeaux at the age of fourteen. She was then engaged by an acting troupe and, having fallen in love with a handsome young actor, embarked for the Caribbean. She then became the mistress of Charles-Martin Hurson, who served as the Intendant of Martinique between 1749 and 1755, and later established her own dress shop on the island of Saint-Domingue—Hispaniola. Upon her return to France, she acquired the support of Marie Antoinette, resulting in the construction of her own theater on the Rue des Réservoirs in Versailles, designed by Jean-François Heurtier (1739-1822). The Théâtre Montansier opened on November 18, 1777, in the presence of Louis XVI and Marie Antoinette. Mademoiselle Montansier died in 1820; her theater is still in operation.

Later that year, the revolutionary government sequestered the properties that Monville had sold to the unfortunate Disney-Ffytche,[179] who had departed for the Helvetic Confederation the previous May 18 along with his daughters, Françoise-Elisabeth and Sophie, their governess Amélie Launnens, their tutor Nicolas Gautherot and Henriette Boulanger, their housemaid.

Since Monsieur de Monville was known to be a collector of clocks, as reported by a visitor to his Grand Hôtel in 1776, and since he was a close friend of Beaumarchais, who had first gained fame as a watchmaker, it is entirely possible that he obtained a timepiece whose face displayed the time in decimal units.

Decimal time owes its origin to the Cahiers de Doléances, lists of grievances drawn upon the orders of Louis XVI to give the French people the chance to express their discontent and their hopes directly to the king. One of the most frequently cited demands was to standardize the system of weights and measures, which varied around the country. The result was the decimal-based Metric System.[180]

---

[179] The Désert was subsequently sold by the town of Chambourcy for 138,000 francs on September 3, 1811, to Jean-Baptiste Lebigre-Beaurepaire. Lewis Disney-Ffytche ultimately recovered the Désert de Retz on February 1, 1816, for a payment of 85,025 francs—settling the claims of Monville's creditors relating to the Désert de Retz—and bequeathed the estate to his daughter.

[180] After returning to the United States, Thomas Jefferson submitted a report to Congress in 1790 in which he proposed the adoption of a decimal system of

In addition to creating standardized units for length, area, volume, and mass, on October 5, 1793 (14 Vendémiaire II), the French abolished the cumbersome Babylonian day of twenty-four hours divided into sixty minutes of sixty seconds each, replacing it with decimal time. In this system, a day is divided into 10 hours of 100 minutes each and each minute contains 100 seconds; thus noon is five o'clock and midnight is ten o'clock. Decimal clocks and watches with dual or multiple dials, some enhanced with revolutionary symbolism and others with the months of the Republican Calendar, were manufactured by renowned horologists such as Jean André Lepaute, Robert Robin and Abraham Louis Breguet. Decimal time proved unpopular, however, and its mandatory use was suspended on April 7, 1795 (18 Germinal III), although the system was maintained in some cities as late as 1801.[181]

Marie Filon Foucaux (1842-1902) was the wife of Philippe Edouard Foucaux (1811-1894), a Tibetologist who published the first Tibetan grammar in French. Writing under the pseudonym Mary Summer and relying on contemporary journals and memoirs, she evokes the atmosphere in ten of the salons frequented by Monsieur de Monville and

---

coinage and of weights and measures. Unfortunately, only decimal coinage was adopted.

[181] Decimal timepieces, including a working clock by master-horologist Antide Janvier are on display at the Conservatoire National des Arts et Métiers and the Musée Carnavalet, both in Paris. Applications for smartphones are available that display both decimal time and the date of the French Republican calendar.

his contemporaries in *Quelques salons de Paris au XVIIIᵉ siècle*, published in 1898.

One chapter is devoted to the salon hosted between 1773 and 1792 by the two Sainte-Amaranthe women, Jeanne-Louise-Françoise de Saint-Simon Desmier d'Archiac (born in 1751), and her daughter Émilie de Sainte-Amaranthe (born in 1775), in their residence on the on the Rue Saint-Anne. [182] Their star-studded guest list included such luminaries as Diderot, d'Alembert, Condorcet the economist and statesman Anne-Robert-Jacques Turgot (1727-1781), the writer Guillaume Thomas Raynal (1713-1796), the historian and writer Jean-Francois Marmontel (1723-1799), the ubiquitous Benjamin Franklin and "the excellent Monville."

Chronicling a soirée in mid-1792, Mary Summer depicts the atmosphere as "frivolity *par excellence*" where, "on the eve of a revolution, the French spirit flourished with inexhaustible verve." She writes that Monville still had enough coins in his change purse to offer his hostesses "a cornet overflowing with bonbons and festooned with scrolls and ribbons."[183]

---

[182] The name was originally Saint-Amarand, but Louis-Barthélémy Davasse de Saint-Amarand, a tax farmer who had gambled away his fortune, abandoned his family and decamped to Spain. He died in 1789. Emilie's mother thereupon feminized the family name to Sainte-Amaranthe. It was also rumored that Emilie's biological father may have been Charles Armand Augustin de Pons (1744-1794), executed along with the membes of the Saint-Amaranthe family

[183] Mary Summers mentions that Monville "wrote verse" while at the Désert de Retz. Perhaps she was only referring to the rhymed lyrics of his songs.

Mary Summer describes another guest, a naval officer known as the Chevalier de Panat,[184] noted for his feminine conquests. He advised one of these ladies to never address him with the *tu* pronoun because, *"le tu est plus familier, mais le vous est plus tendre."*

In one room, many of the thirty guests engaged in conversation, serenaded by 18-year old Émilie on the harp. According to Alexandre de Tilly, Émilie was "more universally famous for her beauty alone than anyone else in France; she was the most beautiful woman of her day; she was beautiful in every respect; I have never, in any country, seen beauty that could be compared with hers, beauty so absolutely perfect." In an adjoining room, some gamblers were engaged in a vigorous game of faro, known in French as *pharaon*, a game of chance in which the players place bets on a card before it is dealt from the deck.

Some of the guests were joking about the newfangled guillotine, which had first been utilized on April 25 of that year. At length, Louis René Quentin de Richebourg de Champcenetz (1759-1794), noted for his sarcasm and his wit, cried out, "While we're waiting for them to cut our heads off, why worry? Let's eat our supper!" Indeed, Champcenetz did embark on a one-way trip to the guillotine on July 24, 1794 (6 Thermidor II), promising the wagoner taking him to the scaffold

---

[184] Léopold de Brunet de Castelpers (1762-1834).

that, if they arrived ahead of time, he would be rewarded with a fat tip.

In 1792, Madame de Sainte-Amaranthe opened a luxurious casino in one of the arcades of the Palais Royal. Numéro 50 was noteworthy for its upper-class clientele, the opulence of its interiors and the excellence of its chef. Monville was one of the patrons and liked to try his luck at Trente Quarante, a card game resembling blackjack, still played in some casinos. Mary Summer observes that, since the gamblers were seated randomly around the gaming tables, on one occasion the "old aristocrat" Monville found himself next to a "young Republican" named Marie-Jean Hérault de Seychelles, who, on his first visit to Numéro 50, broke the bank. Unfortunately, Hérault ran afoul of Robespierre and was accused of treason. He was tried before the Revolutionary Tribunal and condemned along with four others, all of whom were executed on April 5, 1794 (16 Germinal II). As things turned out, the "old aristocrat" kept his head, while the "young Republican" lost his.

Émilie de Sainte-Amaranthe was infatuated with a young operatic tenor named Jean Elleviou (1769-1842), who had a jealous mistress, a *danseuse* named Clotilde Malfleury (1776-1825). Elleviou did not meet with the approval of Emilie's mother, who served notice on her daughter to select without delay a husband from among her more acceptable suitors. Accordingly, in September 1792, Emilie married a wealthy government administrator named Charles

Marie-Antoine de Sartine (1760-1794) although she and Elleviou continued to engage in clandestine trysts at the country home that Emilie's mother had bought with the profits of her casino, the Château de Chaumoncel, in the town of Sucy-en-Brie, southeast of Paris. The carefree Emilie, it is said, "loved to dance on the lawn on Sundays with the farmhands who had not yet begun to detest their masters."

Émilie, along with her husband, her mother, her 17-year old brother Louis (nicknamed Lili), and 50 others, all falsely accused of fomenting a plot against Robespierre, met the same fate on June 17, 1794 (29 Prairial II). In the tumbrel, on their way to the guillotine, Émilie is reported to have remarked on the red sackcloth they had been condemned to wear, "Look, mother, at these red cloaks; we look like the College of Cardinals." The massacre of the 54 innocents lasted all of 28 minutes. Sartine had a habit of seasoning his conversation with lyrical quotations. His last words, addressed to his wife were:

> La mort même est une faveur,
> Puisque le tombeau nous rassemble.[185]

Armandine Rolland reports that an elegantly outfitted Clotilde Malfleury was on hand to "fix her hateful gaze" on the divine face of her unfortunate rival.[186]

---

[185] "Even death does us a favor, for the tomb brings us together."

[186] Dame Fortune spurned Emilie but smiled on both Emilie's lover and her rival. In 1813, at the age of 44, Jean Elleviou left the stage at the acme of his

In *Marat, ou Les Héros de la Revolution*, published in 1883, Léo Taxil and Jean Vindex recount a dinner in the apartments of the Duc d'Orléans—now known as Philippe-Egalité—in the Palais Royal in Paris that took place in mid-October 1792, three months after Monville had sold his properties. There were but three guests: the duke's *maîtresse en titre*, Madame de Buffon (1767-1808),[187] General Charles-François Dumouriez (1739-1823) and Monville, characterized by the authors as a *viveur émérite*—a "pleasure-seeker emeritus."

Conversation was mostly idle chatter and trivialities, interspersed with the ribald yarns that Dumouriez excelled in spinning. As dessert was served, the general noticed that Madame de Buffon appeared melancholy. "I can't stop thinking about the horrible death of that poor Lamballe, six weeks ago; I'm obsessed by her." This lugubrious recollection cast a pall over the festivities, but Monville was the least affected by the narrative. Taxil and Vindex

---

glory, retiring rich and illustrious. He married a "wealthy admirer," bought the Château de Ronzière, near Lyons, began a second career as an agronomist and ended his life a respected public servant. Clotilde Malfleury married the composer François-Adrien Boieldieu in 1802.

[187] Born Marguerite Françoise Bouvier de la Mothe de Cepoy, she married Georges-Louis-Marie Leclerc de Buffon, the son of the renowned naturalist. They were divorced in early 1794, and her husband was executed on the guillotine on July 10, 1794 (22 Messidor II). Her son, born in 1792, was given the name Victor Leclerc de Buffon and did not learn that his biological father was Duc d'Orléans until 1807. Known as the Chevalier de Saint Paul, he served in the English army and died in action in 1812 during the siege of Badajoz, when his leg was shattered by a cannonball.

comment that for the "cynical" Monville, "What counted most was the golden trough in the princely stables where he was feeding."

"Madame," observed Monville drily, "Isn't it best to leave the dead lie in peace?"

"You have a heart of stone," replied Madame de Buffon, "You were not a witness, as the prince and I were, to the horrible spectacle on the third of September. We were seated by one of the windows of the living room overlooking the square and watched a sinister mob approaching. A crazed individual was waving a pike on whose end was impaled a woman's head, its blonde curls fluttering around the blood-soaked staff. We recognized the head of the Princess de Lamballe. Terrified, I cried out, "That's what they'll do with my head one of these days!"

Annoyed, the Duc d'Orléans snapped, "Bah! What good is it to make predictions so far in the future?"

"Monsignor is right," declared Monville.

Madame Buffon's apprehension was misplaced; unlike both her husband and her lover, she outlived the Revolution and died peacefully on May 18, 1808, her head still firmly attached to her body.

Grace Dalrymple Elliott (1758–1823) was a Scots socialite and courtesan resident in Paris at the time of the French Revolution and another mistress of the Duc d'Orléans. Because of her associations with the nobility, she was arrested and imprisoned from December 1793 to October 1794. In her "highly colored, exaggerated and partly fictional" account of her experiences, *During the Reign of Terror: Journal of My Life during the French Revolution,* published posthumously in 1859, she pretended to have shared a cell with Madame du Barry, a claim that was later refuted by the historian Horace Bleakley. What is true is that, unlike Madame du Barry, Grace Elliott survived the Reign of Terror and was released after the death of Robespierre. Her autobiography became the inspiration for a film, *The Lady and the Duke*, by the late director Eric Rohmer.

Monsieur de Monville was the guest of the Duc d'Orléans again on April 6, 1793 (17 Germinal I), as recounted by the Abbé Guillaume-Honoré Rocques Montgaillard (1772-1825) in Tome IV of his *Histoire de France.* Describing Monville as "an epicurean, honored for his kindness, no less than for the delights of the interiors of his residences," the Abbé Montgaillard adds that the Duc d'Orléans often visited Monville at the Désert, which he declared "a masterpiece of art and taste."

As Monville and the duke played cards, servants brought dinner to their table. During the meal, the parliamentarian Merlin de Douai rushed in with the news that the Convention, meeting in the Tuileries

Palace nearby, had issued a warrant to arrest the Duc d'Orléans.

"Great God," the Duc d'Orléans exclaimed, striking his forehead, "After all the proofs of patriotism that I have given, after all the sacrifices that I've made, to deliver such a blow! What ingratitude! How horrible! What say you, Monville?" Monville, who was calmly skinning a filet of sole and drizzling lemon juice over it, replied nonchalantly, "It's appalling, Monsignor, but what do you expect— Your Excellency is of no further use to them and they're doing to you what I've just done to this lemon; I've squeezed out all its juice." And with that, Monville tossed both halves of the lemon into the fireplace and reminded his host that sole was best eaten hot.

The Duc d'Orléans was apprehended along with other members of the Bourbon family on April 7 1793, shortly after his dinner in Monville's company. First imprisoned in Paris, he was then transferred to Fort Saint-Jean in Marseilles and then returned to Paris in October, during the Reign of Terror. Tried and executed on November 6, 1793 (16 Brumaire II), his son, Louis Philippe I (1773-1850), crowned in 1830, was the last king of France.[188]

What historians call the Reign of Terror began on September 5, 1793 (19 Fructidor I) and lasted until July 28, 1794 (10 Thermidor II). It was marked by

---

[188] He lived in exile from 1793 to 1815, including four years in Philadelphia.

mass executions of "enemies of the revolution." The death toll ranged in the tens of thousands, with 16,594 perishing on the guillotine (2,639 in Paris alone), and another 25,000 in summary executions across France.

In the fury of the Reign of Terror, the tax farmers became convenient scapegoats. On November 24, 1793 (4 Frimaire II), the Convention declared the tax farmers to be "enemies of the revolution." Subsequently, thirty former tax farmers were sent to the scaffold, twenty-eight of them on the same day, May 8, 1794 (19 Floréal II).

Lest we think that all the tax farmers were "rapacious and tyrannical," among them was the philosopher and scientist Antoine Lavoisier (1743-1794), who had recognized and named oxygen in 1778 and hydrogen in 1783 and is considered the father of modern chemistry. Lavoisier utilized his profits as a tax farmer to finance his scientific experiments.

It is said that, at his trial, Lavoisier, accused of treason, requested the presiding judge, a young, revolutionary zealot named Jean-Baptiste Coffinhal (1762-1794), to grant him a two-week stay of execution in order to complete an experiment in progress. Coffinhal's purported retort would merit mention in the annals of infamy: "The Republic has no need of either scholars or chemists!" Lavoisier was executed the same day. Less than three months later, however, Coffinhal followed in Lavoisier's footsteps: the ignorant fanatic was guillotined on August 6, 1794 (19 Thermidor II).

As the Reign of Terror was reaching its peak, Monville's position became precarious, and it appears that he found it necessary to avoid detection by the authorities, either by seeking shelter with friends or fleeing Paris. Therefore, we learn that, on May 14, 1793 (25 Floréal I), a residence permit was issued to "Citizen Nicolas Henry [sic] Racine Monville" in Neuilly-sur-Seine. The entry in the registry, which can be consulted in the Neuilly Archives, describes him as "*5 feet 6 inches tall, with chestnut hair and eyebrows, blue eyes, a sharp nose, a small mouth, a round chin, a bare forehead and an oval face*" and adds that he was domiciled in the Porte Maillot neighborhood. A week later, on May 22, a sworn warrant was issued in Paris for Monville's arrest, but he had already decamped to what was presumably a safehouse in Neuilly.

On the same page of the registry appear the names twenty-one year old Vincent Perrot [or Pérot], a native of Saint-Nom-la-Bretèche, "attached" to Jean-Philippe de Franquetot de Coigny (1743-1806), as well as *citoyennes* Marie Cécile Cartier, age 30, and 33-year old Françoise Latreville, both attached to Jeanne Antoinette Thérèse Bouret (1746-1813), the owner of the Château de la Bretèche and the

196

widow of Monville's friend, Denis Thiroux de Montsauge (1715-1786).[189]

Like hundreds of other cities and towns in France whose names bore a religious, royal or aristocratic connotation, the town of Saint-Nom-la-Bretèche was first renamed Montagne-Fromentale and then, L'Union-la-Bretesche during the French Revolution.

The movement had begun as early as 1792, and was officialized by a decree on October 16, 1792 (25 Vendémiaire II); subsequently hundreds of towns and cities across France were renamed. Thus, Saint-Germain-en-Laye became Montagne-du-Bon-Air, Marly-le-Roi was known thenceforth as Marly-la Machine[190] and Versailles was rebaptised Berceau-de-la-Liberté, the Cradle of Liberty.[191]

As early as 1794, however, towns and cities began to change back to their previous names. Although an ordinance of July 8, 1814, formally reëstablished the prerevolutionary toponyms, a few towns resisted and retained their "revolutionary" names: for example, the town known today as Chézy-sur-

---

[189] When Thiroux de Montsauge died, he was in debt to Monville for 100,000 *livres*.

[190] The Machine de Marly, which was actually located in the town of Bougival, was a massive construction completed in 1684 and designed to supply water from the Seine to the fountains at Versailles.

[191] A complete list of the old and new names appears in *Les changements de noms de lieux en 1792-1793*, published by Éditions Archives & Culture in 2012.

Marne was Chézy-l'Abbaye during the Ancien Régime.

After buying time and demonstrating his loyalty by contributing large sums of money as "patriotic gifts" to the revolutionary government, Monsieur de Monville seemed to have successfully avoided capture. On May 17, 1794 (28 Floréal II), however, he was apprehended at the Château de la Bretèche, where he most likely had been sheltered by Jeanne Antoinette Thérèse Bouret, widow of his friend, Denis Thiroux de Montsauge. After his arrest, Monville, accused of the crimes of "anglomania[192] and sybaritism," was imprisoned, first in the Conciergerie in Paris, where Marie Antoinette had awaited her fate, then, apparently because of illness, transferred to a *maison d'arrêt*, the Hôtel Talaru, where the financier Jean-Joseph de Laborde, the owner of the picturesque garden of Méréville, had also been incarcerated until his execution on the 18th of April.

There were sixteen prisons in Paris at that time: the Conciergerie, the oldest, was considered the "antechamber to the guillotine." The living conditions of prisoners varied greatly from one place of detention to another. There were epidemics in the worst prisons.

---

[192] Perhaps "anglomania" indicates that Monville could speak English. There is no proof, but it is certain that he possessed English grammars and dictionaries, received numerous English-speaking guests, including Samuel Johnson, Viscount Powerscourt and Thomas Jefferson, and he sold his real estate to an Englishman.

The number of prisoners during the Reign of Terror is estimated at 500,000. Since the prisons were full, private homes and hospices were requisitioned to take up the overflow. The Marquis César Marie de Talaru et de Chalmazel had been in the service of Marie Antoinette and was a former tax farmer. During the Reign of Terror, he owned two town houses built in 1771, located at numbers 60 and 62 rue de Richelieu [renamed Rue de la Loi]. He rented one of these buildings to a restaurateur named Pierre François Gense and his wife Marie Rosalie Schaff, who wanted to open a hotel; the rent was 7,000 *livres* per trimester.

However, the building was requisitioned by the authorities of the Le Pelletier Section[193] on May 17, 1794, and refurbished as a jail. Talaru himself became its first inmate, confined to a single room in his own house and compelled to pay his captors an extortionate rent of 18 *livres* per day; he had previously charged a rent of just 19 *livres* a day for the whole building!

As many as 200 prisoners were lodged in the building. Among the internees in the Hôtel Talaru was at least one of Monville's personal acquaintances, Jean-Benjamin de La Borde. A former tax farmer and a Freemason, La Borde was a mapmaker and a prolific albeit mediocre composer. The acclaimed dancer Marie-Madeleine Guimard

---

[193] Revolutionary Paris was divided administratively into 48 *section*s; today, Paris comprises 20 *arrondissements*.

was his *maitresse en titre* and the mother of his daughter; Monville had attended the girl's wedding as a witness for the groom.

Another noteworthy detainee was Charles-Robert Boutin (1722-1794), a financier and former Treasurer of the French Navy. He had commissioned Jacques Denis Antoine, the architect of the Paris Mint, to design the elegant neo-classical Château de Herces in Berchères-sur-Vesgre in Normandy.[194]

The heterogeneous list of detainees also included the statesman and financier, Jean-Marie Boscary de Romaine (1746-1797) ; Jeanne de Lavaulx (1734-1815), widow of the Duke of Richelieu; a Protestant pastor, Paul-Henri Marron (1754-1832); son-in-law of the philosopher Claude-Adrien Helvétius, an Alsatian nobleman named Frédéric-Antoine-Marc d'Andlau (1736-1820) and the moralist Philippe-Louis Gérard (1737-1813), former canon of the Church of Saint-Louis-du-Louvre.

A young lawyer, Jean-Baptiste Louis-Joseph Billecocq (1765-1829), incarcerated from July 1, 1794, to August 16, 1794, (29 Thermidor to 13 Messidor II), befriended Monville while in custody. He drafted a detailed account of his internment and the conditions inside the Hôtel Talaru; the document remained in the family archives until it was

---

[194] The Château de Herces is currently the property of an official of Abu Dhabi.

annotated by the historians Nicole Felkay and Hervé Favier and published in 1981 by the Société des Etudes Robespierristes under the title, *En prison sous la Terreur: Souvenirs de J.-B Billecocq*. Favier cites extracts of this account in an article entitled "Angelique Diderot et les Caroillon sous la Révolution" published in 1987 by the Société Française d'Etude du 18ᵉ Siècle. Another contemporary account of the Hôtel Talaru was written by Pierre-Jean-Baptiste Nougaret (1742-1823) in volume 3 of his *Histoire des Prisons de Paris et des départements*, published in 1797. Although a detainee, he does not mention Monville.

According to Billecocq, the detainees were quartered in the various rooms throughout the building. Some, including Monsieur de Monville and Jeanne de Lavaulx, were wealthy enough to pay the exorbitant rents charged to occupy single rooms or individual suites.

Other inmates, less wealthy, had to share rooms converted into dormitories. Felkay and Favier quote Nougaret that a daily rent of 4 francs was charged to share with seven roommates a "beau salon" on the ground floor overlooking the garden.

Billecocq's roommates included a building contractor, the manager of a boarding house, a canon, a "gentleman from the province of Limousin" and an arms dealer.

Billecocq admired and respected Monsieur de Monville, who "so famous for the impression he had once made in polite society, remained just as impressive in jail."

Paraphrasing Billecocq, Favier notes that prisoners could relax in the courtyard, procure their own bedding and, like Monville, order their meals from outside prepared by a caterer. Many shared their provisions and partook of lunch together. Undertaking the chores, they avoided the necessity of prying servants so that they could converse without being overheard. The internees played reversi, whist, piquet or backgammon, paid each other visits and played word games such as *bouts-rimés*. Music also helped them to forget their misfortune. A certain Madame Perthuis, "a consummate artist," played the violin while Joseph-Barthélémy-Clair de Bongars (1762-1833), excelled in accompanying himself on the guitar. Billecocq also notes that he busied himself translating *Voyages Made in the Years 1788 and 1789, from China to the North West Coast of America,* by Captain John Meares, at the request of a Parisian publisher named Buisson.[195]

Aside from their walks in the courtyard, some young people enjoyed a game of badminton. Billecocq observes that Monville perfected his game while awaiting the executioner:

---

[195] Billecocq's translation was published in 1796 and reprinted in facsimile in 2014.

202

"The housekeeping finished, I went back down into the courtyard and, usually, the exercise in which I most frequently indulged was badminton. Boscary proved to be quite good, but he was outplayed by Monville who, despite his age [60 years], retained all the grace, all the address, the elegance of conduct and manners for which he had been so long and so universally praised among the great and the good."

At nine o'clock at night, lights out, followed by unannounced rounds by the jailers, and nights that were undisturbed except on one occasion when, due to a misunderstanding, César Marie Talaru and Charles-Robert Boutin were sent to the scaffold.

The order of the Revolutionary Court was "to summon Jean-Benjamin de La Borde, [who was] housed in Boutin's room, at the Hôtel Talaru." But all three were hauled before the court, whose magistrates found it easier to modify the indictment than release the two innocents! All three were guillotined on July 22, 1794 (4 Thermidor II).

Hervé Favier remarks that this event "dispelled the illusions" born of the *dolce vita* enjoyed in a detention center that was far more comfortable than many others, but where the shadow of death still lurked, omnipresent. Many detainees, once friendly and talkative, sank into sullenness. It was not until the demise of Robespierre that the prisoners' troubled hearts were calmed and most regained their freedom.

On July 28, 1794, less than a week after the execution of La Borde, Boutin and Talaru, the Reign of Terror ended when Robespierre himself was slain by the same "terrible, swift sword" to which he had sent so many innocent victims: the Revolution had devoured its child. Those in prison awaiting execution were exculpated and released from detention. Monsieur de Monville gained his freedom on August 5, 1794 (18 Thermidor II).

The Hôtel Talaru was demolished in 1914 to allow the construction of offices of the Havas advertising agency. The Conciergerie, one of the most popular sites in Paris, continues to attract almost half a million visitors each year.

From this point forward, nothing substantial is known today about François Racine de Monville's activities except that he witnessed the marriage on September 13, 1796 (27 Fructidor IV) between his friend Jeanne Antoinette Thérèse Bouret and Jean-Philippe de Franquetot de Coigny, who had been her devoted suitor for a number of years.

François Nicolas Henri Racine de Monville died while residing in a building located at 64, Rue du Faubourg-Saint-Honoré, in what is now the prestigious Eighth Arrondissement of Paris. The building was owned by a Citizen Berenger, who apparently rented a large apartment to Louis-

Antoine de Rohan-Chabot (1733-1807)[196] who, in turn, sub-let it to Monville for a rent of 2,000 *livres* per year. The cause of Monville's death was an abscessed gum resulting from complications that developed four days after dental surgery. The registry in the Archives of Paris consulted by this author indicates that he died on 19 Ventôse V, corresponding to March 9, 1797, although the inventory of Monville's estate, conducted after his death, reports his death as 18 Ventôse.

The inventory was conducted under the auspices of *Maître* Denis Trutat on 24 Ventôse V (March 14, 1797) and required almost two months to complete, the last entry being dated 17 Floréal V (May 6, 1797). The document[197] is preserved in the French National Archives and consists of over a hundred pages, itemizing the furniture and decorative objects and artwork, clothing, linens, kitchen utensils, wines, books and crockery as well as all of Monville's other personal effects. Each item of furniture and houseware was appraised and its estimated value duly noted by an auctioneer named Jean Girardin. A running total was kept of each item; the grand total amounted to 17,272 *livres* 12 *sols*. The document also contains summaries of some of Monville's

---

[196] The Duc de Rohan-Chabot had borrowed 200,000 *livres* from Madame du Barry to finance an uprising in the Vendée region. He lived in exile from 1790 to 1792; in 1794 his chateau at Pontivy was confiscated and he was forced to sell most of his real estate. He was the father of Alexandrine Charlotte Sophie de Rohan-Chabot, known as Rosalie de la Rochefoucauld, who engaged in a torrid and adulterous love affair with William Short, Jefferson's protégé and successor as American ambassador to France, serving from 1790 to1792.

[197] MC/ET/LVIII/595

personal papers, including the parchment contract of marriage to Aimable Charles Félicité Lucas de Boncourt, details of the sale of his Paris and Chambourcy properties to Lewis Disney-Ffytche, and various other financial transactions. The appraisers were so meticulous that the last page records amounts owed to Monville's apothecary, Citizen Chaumet; two physicians, a hired coachman and a cabinetmaker.

Conducted room by room, the inventory reveals that Monville resided comfortably in spacious and well-appointed quarters overlooking the Rue du Faubourg Saint-Honoré comprising a living room, a dining room, a master bedroom, a kitchen and pantry, a linen closet and several other rooms. Monville also had the use of a wine cellar, and a back staircase led to the quarters for his domestic help, a cook, a valet named Jean-Pierre Dunes and another domestic servant, Nicolas Courtot.

Monville's wine cellar was amply stocked with over 750 bottles and half-bottles, including white wines from the Rhine and Champagne; Médoc and Hermitage red wines and sweet malmsey wines from Cyprus, Madeira and Malaga. Also noted was anisette, *Vin de Hongrie* (presumably Tokaji Aszú) and *Eau des Barbades*, a sweet infusion of lemon peels in alcohol that appears similar to today's Italian limoncello.

The kitchen quite naturally was equipped with an impressive battery of hammered, tin-lined copper cookware including a trout kettle and a lozenge-shaped *turbotière* or turbot poacher.[198]

In the living room, paintings, etchings, engravings, *objets d'art* and other items were recorded. Among the more noteworthy objects:

- Two *quinquets*. These were oil lamps fitted with glass chimneys—the high-tech lighting of the day—perfected by pharmacist Antoine Quinquet (1745-1803). Quinquets, along with candelabra, were found in other rooms.
- A pair of pedestal tables known as *athéniennes,* each with its gilded copper *cassette* for burning incense. [199]
- Five bows and their quivers containing "a great quantity of arrows"
- A "charming landscape representing a picturesque view of the Désert [de Retz] by [Hubert] Robert"
- Two compositions in oil representing seascapes, by Vernet[200]

---

[198] A copper turbot poacher sells today for €349.47 at E. Dehillerin in Paris and $1,975.00 at Williams-Sonoma.

[199] The design was inspired by an artifact discovered at Pompeii. According to Christies, "The multi-purpose *athénienne* was intended for entertaining in the *salon* or *boudoir* and was accordingly fitted with casters and an ormolu-mounted patinated copper cassolette, silvered on the inside and containing a removable spirit lamp."

[200] Claude-Joseph Vernet (1714-1789).

- A landscape painted by Loutherbourg[201]
- Two "copies after Joseph Marie Vien," [202] *La Jeune Corinthienne* and its companion piece, *La Vertueuse Athénienne*
- Sixteen colored landscapes in gouache including "several views of the Désert by different modern artists"
- 24 magic lantern slides in mahogany mounts; the magic lantern itself was stored separately
- *A lunette à long vue*, or spyglass, mounted in a mahogany stand
- One harp and two violins in their cases, as well as a *quinte*, a five-stringed relative of the viola, "in excellent condition"

Also found in the apartment were two violin mutes and four music stands; it therefore seems likely that Monville could have hosted recitals by a chamber quartet.

Among the furniture in the dining room were a *tête-à-tête*, or love seat, and an oval *rafraichissoire à vin*, a wine table in mahogany equipped with plated lead wells for chilling two bottles of wine at a time.

The lot with the highest appraised value was silver tableware hallmarked by the Paris silversmiths: forks, teaspoons, tablespoons, soupspoons, sugar

---

[201] Philip James de Loutherbourg (1740-1812) was born in Strasbourg but lived and worked in England, were he died.

[202] Joseph Marie Vien (1716-1809), was the last *Premier peintre du roi*. He is the only painter buried in the Pantheon.

spoons, basting spoons and a *cuillère à olives*, perforated like an absinthe spoon to filter out the brine. The total weight of the silverware came to 32 *marcs*, [203] corresponding to 16 pounds or 7.83 kilograms, and was appraised at 1,621 *livres* 12 *sols*, almost one-tenth of the value of the entire estate.

Monville's extensive wardrobe included an outfit in grey vicuña, [204] a silk taffeta greatcoat, a dozen waistcoats in yellow cotton nankeen, 25 silk muslin neckties, 45 "threadbare shirts" and an overcoat woven in *castorine,* a fabric blending wool and beaver fur that was certainly both warm and waterproof.

In the bedroom was a *fontaine à thé* or samovar, and in a small room behind the bedroom, a *chaise de commodité*, an elegant term for *chaise percée*, known in English as a "privy chair" or "commode."

The cataloguing of 180 lots of books in Monville's library was undertaken by François-Hubert Monory (17?-1805), a bookseller with a shop in the *faubourg* of Saint-Germain-des-Prés on the Left Bank, and commenced on 2 Floréal V (April 21, 1797). The collection consisted of volumes in folio, quarto, octavo and duodecimo and most were sets bound in morocco leather. Many of the lots contained more

---

[203] The *marc* was a unit of mass dating from the mid-13ᵗʰ century, equivalent to eight ounces or 244.7 grams.

[204] Vicuña is the world's rarest cloth. An Ermenegildo Zegna vicuña sports coat costs approximately $21,000.

than one tome—the *Encyclopédie* by Diderot and d'Alembert alone comprises 45 volumes—thus the total number of books in Monville's library could have easily reached a thousand, a substantial private collection for its day.[205]

The entire collection of Monsieur de Monville's Paris library appears to have been sold as one, then broken up and reassembled, since most of the books are listed in 325 lots in an undated, thirty-page brochure entitled *Notice des Livres, Après le Décès de Racine Montville* [*sic*] listing their titles, authors, publication dates and dimensions and which may have served as the catalogue for their sale. The Bodleian Library in Oxford, England, possesses a copy of this brochure, which may be consulted on line; a facsimile edition has been published and is available from booksellers. One item from Monville's library, a four volume folio edition of La Fontaine's *Fables*, stamped in gold with Monville's *super libros* on the front covers, fetched €8,500 at an auction conducted by Alde in Paris on October 17, 2009.

Along with the inventories of Monsieur de Monville's personal effects at the Désert de Retz and Paris, the contents of his library offer many insights into his interests and passions

---

[205] In 1815, Thomas Jefferson sold to Congress his collection of 6,487 books, the largest personal library in America, for $23,950.

Monville designed both his residences in Paris and the buildings at the Désert de Retz in Chambourcy, therefore books about architecture and manuals on design comprise a significant part of the collection. Drama, not only the works of the French 17th and 18th century playwrights, but translations from the Greek and Latin classics—both comedies and tragedies—are also much in evidence; some of these plays, or excerpts thereof, were certainly performed at Monville's Open-air Theater. The collection also contains a large selection of novels, a form of literature that originated in the mid-eighteenth century. Monville owned not only many novels by French authors, but works by Samuel Richardson, Henry Fielding, Jonathan Swift and Daniel Defoe, many of them translated by the Abbé Antoine François Prévost (1697-1763), author of the controversial novel *Manon Lescault*.

Although Monville's proficiency in English is unknown, he owned a pocket dictionary of English along with a grammar and an English spelling dictionary. In addition to translations of numerous English novelists, Monville also possessed collections of poetry by John Milton and Alexander Pope and a complete bound collection in eight volumes of *The Spectator*, the daily newspaper edited by Joseph Addison and Richard Steele and published between 1711 and 1712.

Many books on ethics, morals, religion and philosophy are found in the collection, ranging from the Holy Bible, a *Vie de Mahomet* and a *Histoire des*

Juifs translated from the works of Titus Flavius Josephus, to the *Histoire de la Papesse Jeanne*, the story of the legendary female pope who is supposed to have given birth while riding on horseback, after which she was lapidated.

It has been suggested that Monville was interested in occultism and may even have used his laboratory at the Désert de Retz to conduct experiments in alchemy. These speculations are supported to some extent by the fact that items 31 through 33 on the *Notice* include titles in Latin and French relating to magic and occultism as well as *Les Vraies Centuries & Prophéties de Nostradamus*.

One of the most interesting items was a 33-volume collection of the works of Jean-Baptiste de Boyer, Marquis d'Argens (1704-1771), including *Lettres Juives*, *Lettres Chinoises*, and *Lettres Cabalistiques*, a trilogy of satirical epistolary novels inspired by Montesquieu's *Lettres Persanes*. The fictionalized correspondents—rabbis, a Chinese traveler and cabalists—dissect and critique organized religions and government institutions in various countries. [206]

The Marquis d'Argens was an atheist who, after an adventurous youth, was disowned by his father. After spending time in Amsterdam, where he wrote and published prolifically, he was invited to the court of Frederick the Great and moved to Berlin in

---

[206] All these works have been reprinted in facsimile and can be purchased at booksellers.

1742, and undertook several missions to Paris and Provence. During one trip, in 1747, he met a beautiful German actress, Babette Cochois (1723-1780) whom he married and with whom he had a daughter, Barbe. He returned definitely to France in 1769. Argens may have befriended Monsieur de Monville in France or in Berlin, since it is reported by Armandine Rolland that Monville played flute in Frederick's orchestra at Sanssouci during the early 1750's.

When we consider important collections of Paris and Chambourcy, it seems clear that Monsieur de Monville was an avid bibliophile. It will, therefore, not surprising to discover that Antoine Caillot (1759-c.1839), a writer, bookseller and freemason from Lyon, inserted a "Monsieur Monville" in his curious "bibliographic" novel, *Voyage autour de ma Bibliothèque*, published in 1809.

The novel is written in first person. A few years after the Revolution, the narrator, Valcourt, heir to the large library of his late uncle, invites two charming young widows, Madame de Cléri and Madame de Gourville, to undertake a bookish journey during which he proposes to compose a list of fifty literary works recommended for the weaker sex. The trio was soon joined by a friend of Valcourt, Monsieur Monville.

The four adventurers roam and comment on the writings of ancient and modern authors, including poets, playwrights, historians and explorers. Each guest also proposes a favorite book. The choice of Madame de Gourville is *Orlando Furioso* by Ludovico Ariosto, Monville prefers Homer's *Iliad*, Valcourt chooses Virgil's *Æneid* and Madame de Cléri *Jerusalem Delivered*, the obscure epic poem by Torquato Tasso inspired by the First Crusade.

In one passage, Caillot writes that his Monville made Valcourt understand that, "to appreciate foreign poets and take pleasure in reading their books, it was essential to learn their language," adding, "It is not in these translations no matter how faithful they be that you will find the genius and delicacy of the originals." Elsewhere, Valcourt remarks to his friend, "Blame all you want the poet Jacques Delille; his works will always be my delight, beginning with his poem *Les Jardins*." Indeed, it is in this poem that Delille includes in a list the real Monville's Désert de Retz! Caillot's Monville, after hearing Valcourt's arguments in favor of the poet, confesses that "It is your moderation that reconciles me with Monsieur Delille."

All this learned conversation is littered with unexpected and, occasionally, comical events: Monville develops a painful limp after the fall of a large folio on his foot; he faints during a storm after being blinded by a flash of lightning. From time to time the voyagers disembark in Valcourt's garden to enjoy a snack served by Marthon, his servant.

Perhaps intoxicated by the fragrances of the printed page, love blooms in the bookshelves: Valcourt falls for Madame de Gourville and Monville for Madame de Cléri. The feelings are mutual; everyone decides to celebrate a double wedding. At this point, the executor of Valcourt's uncle's estate arrives *deus ex machina* to announce that Valcourt has inherited not only the library but also a significant amount of gold, jewels and annuities. The quartet of lovers decides that after the wedding, they will live under the same roof and take their meals together. Valcourt proposes to engage its Monville as his custodian and librarian.

Of course, Caillot's Monville is fictional; however, it is possible that Caillot had known the real Monville and was content to recount some embellished anecdotes. It is also quite possible that choosing "Monville" to designate one of the bibliophiles in his novel was purely fortuitous. Nevertheless, it is intriguing to note the bookish erudition and verve of Caillot's Monville are not so different from those of the real Monville.

Since Monsieur de Monville had no known progeny, the proceeds of his estate were bequeathed to his three great-grandnieces and his great-grandnephew, all of whom were minors and represented by guardians. Marie Stéphanie's two surviving children, Jacqueline Stéphanie de Choiseul-Stainville and Antoine Clériadus de Choiseul-Stainville, and the two daughters of Françoise-Thérèse, Princesses

Honorine Camille Grimaldi and Athénaïse Euphrasie Grimaldi, each inherited an equal portion of the estate. Little is known of any of them except that Jacqueline Stéphanie, married to Philippe Gabriel de Marmier, "led a life as a coquette as long as she could attract lovers," according to the *Journal* of the writer and adademician Xavier Marmier. Numerous descendants of Honorine and Jacqueline are living today; Antoine Clériadus and Athénaïse died childless.

Although we do not know any other names for Sarah, [207] Eugène Hugot, writing in his *Histoire littéraire, critique et anecdotique du Théâtre du Palais-Royal 1784-1885*, published in 1886, states that an "admirably attractive" actress who went by the name of Sarah made her stage debut as "an excellent comedienne" at the age of twelve in a one-act comedy entitled *La Belle Esclave, ou Valcour et Zélia* by Antoine-Jean Bourlin, known as Dumaniant (1752-1828), with music by the composer François-André Danican Philidor (1726-1795), who was also the best chess-player of his day. The play premiered at the Théâtre des Petits Comédiens on September 18, 1787. If Sarah was twelve at the time, she would have been born around 1775.

Hugot also states that an actress named Sarah was married to the Italian operatic tenor and composer

---

[207] It is possible that the names could be determined by consulting the employment records of the theaters where she acted.

Bernardo Mengozzi (1758-1800), who performed both in the Théâtre Montansier in Versailles and the at the Théâtre de Monsieur in Paris, adding that Madame Mengozzi was the mother of Madame Guillemin, "who shone so brightly at the Théâtre du Vaudeville and was unmatched in playing *duègnes*, comical old ladies, on the Paris stage."

According to the entry for Mengozzi in the *Biographie universelle et portative des contemporains*, published in 1826, Sarah Mengozzi continued her stage career after her marriage, appearing at both the Théâtre Montansier and the Théâtre des Variétés in Paris until her retirement in 1808. She was admired for "her pretty face, her decent, graceful manners, and her dulcet voice."

Henry Lyonnet cites in his *Dictionnaire de comédiens français: biographie, bibliographie, iconograph*ie the memoirs first published in 1845 of François-Flore Corvée (1790-1853), a popular actress known as Mademoiselle Flore, who describes Sarah as "graceful" with "very shapely features. [208]

Writing in his memoirs, Dufort de Cheverny observed unkindly, "[Monville] and I knew each other intimately, but he was not a friend, since such

[208] Armandine Rolland, whose book was published in 1864, also notes that a "delicious actress" named Sarah, from Mademoiselle Montansier's company, married a "Monsieur Mangozzi [sic]."

a perfect egotist can have no friends...He had squandered all his money down to the last penny and died a debtor. After being abandoned by all the girls who had populated his one-night-stands, he lived for the last six years with a young actress [Sarah] who performed in small-scale productions."

If Dufort's account is accurate, Monville and Sarah would have started living together around 1791. He was mistaken, however, about the date and place of Monville's birth, and he may also have erred with respect to Monville's death. Although he claims that Monville "died a debtor," perhaps, he was expressing his jealousy and thinking of himself since, like many others, he had been ruined due to the depreciation of his investments, certainly a consequence of the hyperinflation of the *assignats*.

It is the belief of this author and others that, thanks to his close association with Perregaux, Monville probably succeeded in transferring a sizeable part of his net worth outside of France. Consequently, Monville was not impecunious in his later years, but most likely enjoyed a fairly comfortable existence as a *rentier*, living off the proceeds of his investments.

In contrast to Dufort de Cheverny, Alexandre de Tilly penned a more generous tribute to his departed friend: "In surviving the Revolution...Monville found the secret to die peacefully in his bed and to obtain the grace of the French Sylla and Marius,[209] who were not accustomed to according such favors to anyone."

Because of the absence of written records, it can not be determined with absolute certainty where François Racine de Monville was buried. Nevertheless, the Errancis Cemetery was located between the current Boulevard de Courcelles, Rue de Rocher, Rue de Monceau and Rue de Miromesnil in Paris and utilized from March 5, 1793, to April 23, 1797. Between March 1794 and May 1795, 1,119 victims of the guillotine were inhumed there.[210] Subsequently, from August 1796 to its closure, the cemetery received the bodies of persons having resided in the area of Paris where Monville was living. Since Monville died a month before the Errancis Cemetery was closed, it is probable that this is where he was laid to rest.[211]

In 1815, Louis XVIII, a brother of Louis XVI, seeking the remains of his sister, Princess Elisabeth of France (1764-1794), a victim of the guillotine believed transported there, ordered the area to be excavated, but identification was impossible since

---

[209] A reference to the opposing leaders in the Second Roman Civil War, 82 B.C.

[210] The bodies of Robespierre and his partisans were buried in the Errancis Cemetery on July 28, 1794.

[211] A plaque at 97, Rue de Monceau, commemorates the victims of the guillotine interred in the Errancis Cemetery.

the decapitated corpses had been stripped of their clothing before inhumation by the gravediggers who sold the victims' personal effects to bystanders.

Between 1844 and 1859, during the construction of the Boulevard de Courcelles, all the remains in the Errancis Cemetery were transported to the Catacombs of Paris, the underground ossuary occupying an area of 11,000 square meters of ancient quarries, whose entrance is in one of the former city gates, the Barrière d'Enfer, designed by Ledoux in 1787 and located on the Place Denfert-Rochereau, in the Fourteenth Arrondissement of Paris.

It is therefore probable that, today, the mortal remains of François Racine de Monville, the forgotten luminary of the French Enlightenment, lie commingled anonymously in the Catacombs with those of six million of the other unremembered dead.

Appendix

Épitre à Mon Ami

Cher Monville, apprends-moi quelle heureuse magie
Soumet à tes plaisirs, les arts, les tons, les goûts,
Quoique divers entre eux, on les voit s'unir tous
Pour obéir à ton génie.

Un instant développe à ton œil pénétrant
Un talent étranger dont tu fais ton talent.
Ton ingénieuse industrie
Vient à bout sans effort, et même en te jouant
De la plus abstraite entreprise.
Heureux mortel, phénomène vivant,
Apprends-moi donc quel dieu te favorise.

Tu servis autrefois l'impérieux l'enfant
Qui règne sur toute la terre.
Tu le traitas, dit-on, très cavalièrement.
Un système aussi téméraire
Méritait de sa part un juste châtiment.
J'admire ton bonheur, ton audace sut plaire.

Ce dieu que tu brusquais n'en fut que plus charmant.
Il parsema de fleurs chaque instant de ta vie.
Le plaisir qui le suit, sur tes pas voltigeant
Mit bientôt dans tes bras, Fanny, Loÿs, Sylvie.
Trompé par elles et les trompant,
Jouir fut ta philosophie.
Notre maître Épicure en a fait tout autant.

Depuis ce temps, un Dieu plus sévère et décent,
Ami, te mène enfin en triomphe à sa suite.
À son aspect peu caressant
Souvent le tendre Amour soupire et prend la fuite.
Mais de la jeune Églé, la beauté, la conduite
Ont arrêté ce dieu charmant.
En sa faveur, Hymen est devenu galant.

Les jeux, les rires, troupe chérie
S'empresse à former sa cour.
Les grâces auprès d'elle ont fixé leur séjour
Et je sais que Vénus, la voyant accomplie,
A dit en rougissant d'un peu de jalousie :
« Quoi ! Ne suis-je donc plus la mère de l'Amour ? »

Il n'est plus temps que ton désir chancelle
Ami, crois-moi, tu possèdes un trésor
Que l'on n'acquiert pour argent, ni pour or.
Rends grâce aux dieux qui la firent si belle
Et la douèrent à l'envie.
Jouis de tout, mais n'aimes qu'elle.
Tu devras ton bonheur aux conseils d'un ami.

Unis à ces plaisirs les arts que tu cultives
Ne deviens-tu pas professeur
Avec autant de qualités actives ?
De tous les biens de l'esprit et du cœur
Gardes toi d'éplucher mes rimes redoublées,
Mes syllabes peut-être au hasard enfilées.

J'invoque ton Phébus lorsque le cœur écrit
La plume court toujours, l'amitié la conduit

--*Pierre-Augustin Caron de Beaumarchais*

Bibliography

- Adams, William Howard, *The French Garden 1500-1800*, New York, George Braziller, 1979.

- Alger, John Goldsworth, *Paris in 1789-94: Farewell Letters of Victims of the Guillotine*, New York, James Pott & Co., 1902.

- Barère de Vieuzac, Bertrand, "Promenades Pittoresques dans le Parc et Jardin de Betz Rédigées en Forme de Lettres," in *Polia, Revue de l'Art des Jardins*, No. 6, Automne 2006.

- Beaumarchais, Pierre-Augustin Caron de, *Lettre de Beaumarchais à Goursaut, suivie de trois pièces de vers : «Consultation sur l'effet du bouquet à Manon Silvie», « Épitre à mon amy»* [Cher Monville...], *«Romance»* [Comme j'aimais mon ingrate maitresse...]. Manuscript, n.d.

- Beaurepaire, Pierre-Yves, *Nobles jeux de l'Arc et loges maçonniques dans la France des Lumières- Enquête sur une sociabilité en mutation*, Éditions Ivoire-Clair, 2002.

- Bénilan, Christian, *Paris autrefois : Les merveilles disparus du Moyen Age à la Belle Epoque*, Paris, Massin, 2006.

- Billecocq, Jean Baptiste Louis Joseph, *Souvenirs de J.-B Billecocq*, Paris, Société des études Robespierristes, 1981.

- Blanc, Olivier, *Les Libertines*, Paris, Perrin, 1997.

- ---, *L'Amour à Paris au temps de Louis XVI*, Paris, Perrin, 2002.

- Blanchard, Jean-Pierre, *Journal of My Forty-fifth Ascension, Being the First Performed in America...*, Tarrytown, NY, William Abbatt, 1918.

- ---, *Journal and Certificates on the Fourth Voyage of Mr. Blanchard*, London, Baker and Galabin, 1784.

- Bongie, Laurence L., *From Rogue to Everyman: A Foundling's Journey to the Bastille*, Montreal, McGill-Queen's University Press, 2004.

- Boysse, Ernest, *Les Abonnés de l'Opéra (1783-1786)*, Paris, A. Quantin, 1881.

- Broquet, Patrick and Malnic, Evelyne, *Folies de jardin : art et architecture des fabriques de jardin du XVIIIè siècle à nos jours*, Paris Les Éditions du Chêne, 1996.

224

- Burnell, Carol, *Divided Affections: The Extraordinary Life of Maria Cosway*, Column House, Switzerland, 2007.

- Cardinal, Catherine, *La Révolution dans la Mesure du Temps : Calendrier Républicain, Heure Décimale 1793-1805*, La Chaux de Fonds, Musée International d'Horlogerie, 1989.

- Cendres, Julien and Radiguet, Chloé, *Le Désert de Retz, paysage choisi*, Paris, Éditions de l'Éclat, 2009.

- Césari, Dominique, *Les jardins des Lumières en Ile-de-France*, Paris, Parigramme, 2005.

- Choppin de Janvry, Olivier, *Le Désert de Retz : Réponses à 101 questions sur le Désert de Retz*, Croissy-sur-Seine, Société Civile du Désert de Retz, 1998.

- ---, "Le Désert de Retz," in *Le Vieux Marly*, Tome III, No. 3, 1968-1969.

- Connolly, Cyril, and Zerbe, Jerome, *Les Pavillons: French Pavilions of the Eighteenth Century*, London, Hamish Hamilton, 1962.

- Corborand, François, *Inventaire du Désert de Retz*, 1-15 Nivôse II [December 21, 1793-January 4, 1794]. Manuscript.

- Darnton, Robert, "Paris: The Early Internet," in *New York Review of Books*, June 29, 2000.

- Dawson, Warrington, "Les 2,112 Français morts aux Etats-Unis de 1777 à 1785 en combattant pour l'indépendance américaine," in *Journal de la Société des Américainistes*, Volume 28, Number 1, 1936.

- Dietz, Paula, "The Désert de Retz, Near Paris," in *Antiques*, March 1989.

- Duhem, Jules, *Histoire des idées aéronautiques avant Montgolfier*, Paris, Fernand Sorlot, 1943.

- Elliott, Grace Dalrymple, *Journal de Ma Vie Durant la Révolution Française*, Paris, Les Éditions de Paris, 2001. Preface by Eric Rohmer.

- Favier, Hervé, "Angélique Diderot et les Caroillon sous la Révolution," in *Dix-Huitième Siècle*, No 19, Paris, Société française d'Étude du 18e siècle, 1987.

- Furstenberg, François, *When the United States Spoke French: Five Refugees Who Shaped a Nation*, New York, Penguin Press, 2014.

- Gruyer, François-Anatole, *Les Portraits de Carmontelle : Chantilly*, Chantilly, Éditeur scientifique, 1902.

- Harris, John, *Echoing Voices: More Memories of a Country House Snooper*, London, John Murray, 2002.

- Heimbürger Ravalli, Minna, *Disegni di giardini e opere minori di un artista del '700 Francesco Bettini*, Firenze, Olschki Editore, 1981.

- Henri-Deligny, "Lewis Disney Ffytche et sa Maison au Désert de Retz," in *Revue de l'Histoire de Versailles et de Seine-et-Oise*, Avril-Juin 1932.

- Hugot, Eugène, *Histoire littéraire, critique et anecdotique du Théâtre du Palais-Royal, 1784-1884*, Paris, Ollendorff, 1886.

- Humbert, Jean-Marcel, "Egypt in the eighteenth-century garden: decline or revival of the initiatory journey?" in *Experiencing the Garden in the Eighteenth Century*, Oxford, Peter Lang, 2006.

- Hunt, John Dixon and Conan, Michael, editors, *Tradition and Innovation in French Garden Art: Chapters of a New History*, Philadelphia, University of Pennsylvania Press, 2002.

- Isaacson, Walter, *Benjamin Franklin: An American Life*, New York, Simon & Schuster, 2003.

- J. de C., *Les Charmes de Stow*, London, 1748, in *Descriptions of Lord Cobham's Gardens at Stowe,*

1700-1750, edited by G. B. Clarke,
Buckinghamshire Record Society, 1990.

- Jouve, Daniel, *Paris: Birthplace of the U.S.A.*,
Paris, Gründ, 2006.

- Kenyon, Ronald W., "Was Monsieur de
Monville a Freemason? Monsieur de Monville
était-il franc-maçon?," in *La Gazette du Désert de
Retz*, No. 3, June 2011, pages 2-4.

- Ketcham, Diana, "Jefferson's Paris," in
American Heritage Magazine, April 1995, Volume
46, Issue 2. "

- ---,"Amid the Follies, Jefferson Dallied," in *New
York Times*, March 16, 1995

- ---, *Le Désert de Retz: A Late Eighteenth-Century
French Folly Garden – The Artful Landscape of
Monsieur de Monville*, The MIT Press, 1997.

- Kimball, Marie Goebel, "William Short,
Jefferson's Only 'Son,'" in *The North American
Review*, September, 1926.

- ---, *Jefferson: The Scene of Europe 1784-1789*,
Coward-McCann, 1950.

- Landriani, Marsilio, *Dell'utilità dei conduttori
elettrici,* Milan, Marelli, 1784.

• Lécuyer, Raymond and Moreux, Jean-Charles, "Le Désert de M. de Monville," in *L'Amour de L'Art*, Number 3, April 1938.

• Lefèvre, Louis-Eugène, "Le jardin anglais et la singulière habitation de Monville au Désert de Retz," in *Bulletin de la Commission des Antiquités et des Arts de Seine-et-Oise*, XXXVIᵉ Volume, Versailles, Cerf, 1916.

• Lenotre, G. [Louis Léon Théodore Gosselin] *Le Jardin de Picpus*, Paris, Librairie Académique Perrin, 1955.

• Leroux-Cesbron, Charles, "M. de Monville, Propriétaire à Neuilly au XVIIIᵉ Siècle," in *Bulletin de la Commission municipale historique & artistique de Neuilly-sur-Seine*, 1912.

• ---, *Le Château de Neuilly: Chronique d'un Château Royal*, Paris, Perrin, 1923.

• *Les changements de noms de lieux en 1792-1793*, Paris, Éditions Archives & Culture, 2012.

• Letcher, Piers, *Eccentric France*, St Peter, Bucks, Bradt Travel Guides Ltd., 2003.

• Lever, Maurice, *Pierre-Augustin Caron de Beaumarchais Tome I: L'Irrésistible Ascension*, Paris, Fayard, 1999.

- Lopez, Claude-Anne, *Mon Cher Papa: Franklin and the Ladies of Paris*, New Haven, Yale University Press, 1990.

- Lyonnet, Henry, *Dictionnaire de comédiens français: biographie, bibliographie, iconographie*, Geneva, Revue Universelle International Illustrée, 1912.

- Macon, Gustave, *Les Jardins de Betz*, Senlis, Imprimerie Eugène Dufresne, 1908.

- Malet, Tina, *Une vie de Tilly, ou la mort du Lys*, Paris, Edilivre, 2013.

- McCullough, David, *John Adams*, Simon & Schuster, 2002.

- Miller, Melanie Randolph, *Envoy to the Terror: Gouverneur Morris and the French Revolution*, Washington, Potomac Books, 2005.

- *Notice de Livres, Après le Décès de Racine Montville* [sic], n .d.

- Nougaret, Pierre-Jean-Baptiste, *Histoire des Prisons de Paris et des départements*, Tome 3, Paris, 1797.

- Olausson, Magnus, "Freemasonry, Occultism and the Picturesque Garden towards the End of the Eighteenth Century," in *Art History*, 1985.

- ---, "The Désert de Retz Revisited," in *Art Bulletin of Nationalmuseum Stockholm*, Volume 21, Stockholm, 2014.

- Pelay, Édouard, "Pierre Blanchard, aéronaute; histoire de ses ascensions," in *Bulletin des amis des monuments rouennais*, Rouen, Imprimerie Julien Lecerf, 1899.

- Pérouse de Montclos, J.-P., *Etienne-Louis Boullée*, Paris, A. N. G., 1969.

- Popkin, Jeremy D., editor, *Panorama of Paris: Selections from Le Tableau de Paris by Louis-Sébastien Mercier*, University Park, PA, The Pennsyvania State University Press, 1999.

- Rabbe, Alphonse, *et al*, *Biographie universelle et portative des contemporains*, Paris, Levrault, 1836.

- Racine, Claude and Denis, "François-Nicolas-Henry Racine, Baron de Monville (1734-1797)," in *L'Enraciné*, Volume 11, Numéro 1, Hiver 1998.

- Renard, P.-E, "Monsieur de Monville - Homme Sans Visage, Reflet d'une Société," in *Petit journal de l'exposition* (No.4), Louveciennes, Musée Promenade Marly-le-Roi Louveciennes, 1988.

- Rice, Howard C., *Thomas Jefferson's Paris*, Princeton, NJ, Princeton University Press, 1991.

- Rivkin, Jessica, "The Lawyer and the Lightning Rod," in *Science in Context* Volume 12, Issue 1 (1999).

- Robin, Pierre-Ernest-Marie, *Le Séquestre des biens ennemis sous la Révolution française*, Paris Éditions Spes, 1929.

- Robinson, John Martin, *Temples of Delight: Stowe Landscape Gardens*, The National Trust, 1990.

- Rolland, Armandine, *La Famille Sainte-Amaranthe*, Paris, V. Goupy, 1864.

- Rosenblum, Robert, *Transformations in Late Eighteenth Century Art*, Princeton, NJ, Princeton University Press, 1969.

- Saury, Jean-Louis, *Le Désert de Retz-Jardin des Lumières*, Chambourcy, 2009.

- Stinchcombe, William C., *The American Revolution and the French Alliance*, Syracuse, Syracuse University Press, 1969.

- Summer, Mary (Marie Filon Foucaux), *Quelques salons de Paris au XVIIIe siècle*, Paris, L.-H. May, 1898.

- Taxil, Léo, and Vindex, Jean, *Marat, ou Les Héros de la Révolution*, Paris, Librairie Anticléricale, 1883.

- Thiéry, Luc-Vincent, *Guide des amateurs et des étrangers voyageurs à Paris,* Tome Premier, Paris, Hardouin & Gattey, 1787.

- Trutat, Denis *et al, Inventaire après le Décès de Racine de Monville,* 24 Ventôse-17 Floréal V [March 14-May 6, 1797]. Manuscript.

- Vacant, Claude, *Jean-Rodolphe Perronet (1708-1794),* Paris, Presses de l'École Nationale des Ponts et Chaussées, 2006.

- Vidler, Anthony, *The Writing of the Walls: Architectural Theory in the Late Enlightenment*, Princeton, NJ, Princeton Architectural Press, 1987.

- Waquet, Jean-Claude, *Les Grands maîtres des eaux et forêts de France de 1689 à la Révolution*, Genève, Droz, 1978.

- White, Eugene N., *France's Slow Transition from Privatized to Government-Administered Tax Collection: Tax Farming in the Eighteenth Century*, New Brunswick, NJ, Rutgers University, 2001.

Index

238

241

244

245

About the Author

Ronald W. Kenyon was born and raised in Ashland, Kentucky. He graduated from the University of Michigan, Ann Arbor, where he specialized in English literature, political science and Spanish and was awarded Avery Hopwood awards in creative writing for poetry and drama. He completed his graduate studies at Stanford after receiving a Woodrow Wilson National Fellowship and at Saint Lawrence University under a National Defense Education Act scholarship. He was certified as a French-English liaison interpreter by the U.S. Department of State Office of Language Services.

Since 2012, he has published collections of poetry, essays and photography. A French translation of this biography of François Racine de Monville is available under the title *Monville: l'inconnu des Lumières.*

Ronald W. Kenyon developed an interest in photography at a young age. During the nineteen-seventies, when he was living in Paris, he experimented with numerous camera systems including the Rolleiflex, Leica and Nikon. He participated in a three-person show at the Galerie Noir-et-Blanc in Paris in November 1976, the 5th Salon d'Art Photographique in Rambouillet in 1977 and the Exposition "Camera" in Versailles in January 1978. His photography was awarded the

Grand Prix by the Société Artistique of Fontenay-le-Fleury in 1977. In January 1980 he was chief photographer for a project to document traditional architecture in Asir Province, Saudi Arabia. Sixty-five of his photographs were exhibited at the First International Symposium on Islamic Architecture and Urbanism at King Faisal University in Dammam.

Although nominally retired, Ronald W. Kenyon continues his writing and photography; projects in both areas are in progress.

Also by Ronald W. Kenyon

Divagations: Collected Poetry 1959-1996
A Winter in the Middle of Two Seas: Real Stories from Bahrain
Monville: l'inconnu des Lumières
Le Petit Kenyon: Dining in the Environs of Paris for Walkers
Statues of Liberty: Real Stories from France
On the Trail in France
Floridians: Real Stories from the Sunshine State

Photography

Metro Portraits
Metro Messages
My Beautiful France: Landscapes
Ile-de-France, terres d'inspiration
France Images & Messages

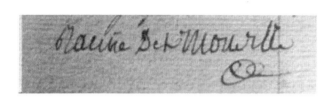

July 30, 2016
13 Thermidor CCXXIV
51168

253

Printed in Great Britain
by Amazon